To all the young dreamers and artists, may your imagination always be as boundless as the stars and your creations as magical as the creatures within these pages. This book is dedicated to you, with love and wonder.

MY NAME IS :

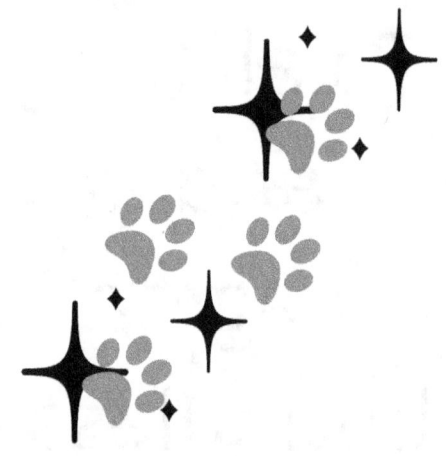

_____

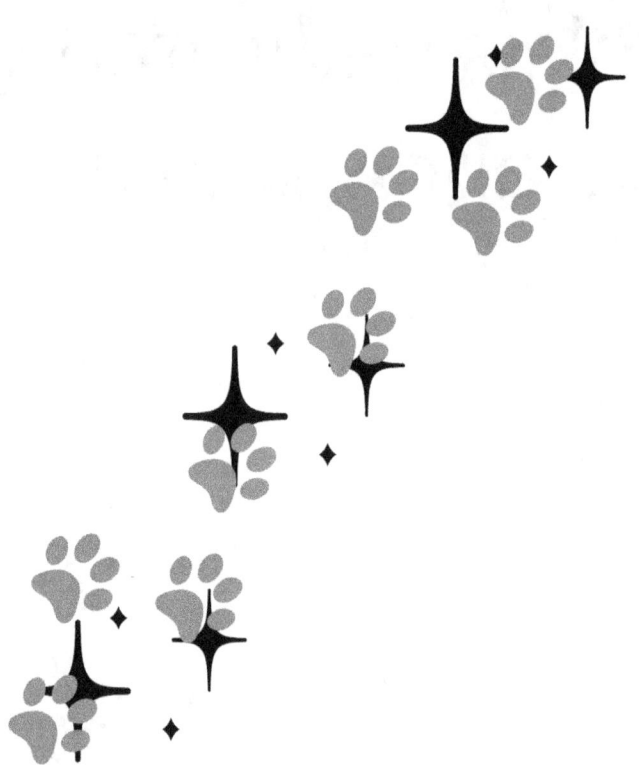

ALL RIGHTS RESERVED©
2024

No part of this publication may be reproduced, distributed, or transmitted in any form or by any means, including photocopying, recording, or other electronic or mechanical methods, without the prior written permission of the publisher, except for brief quotations incorporated in critical reviews and other specific noncommercial uses. Any unauthorized replica of this work is prohibited.

L.P.T©
Lara Perguer Tramontin

Test color page

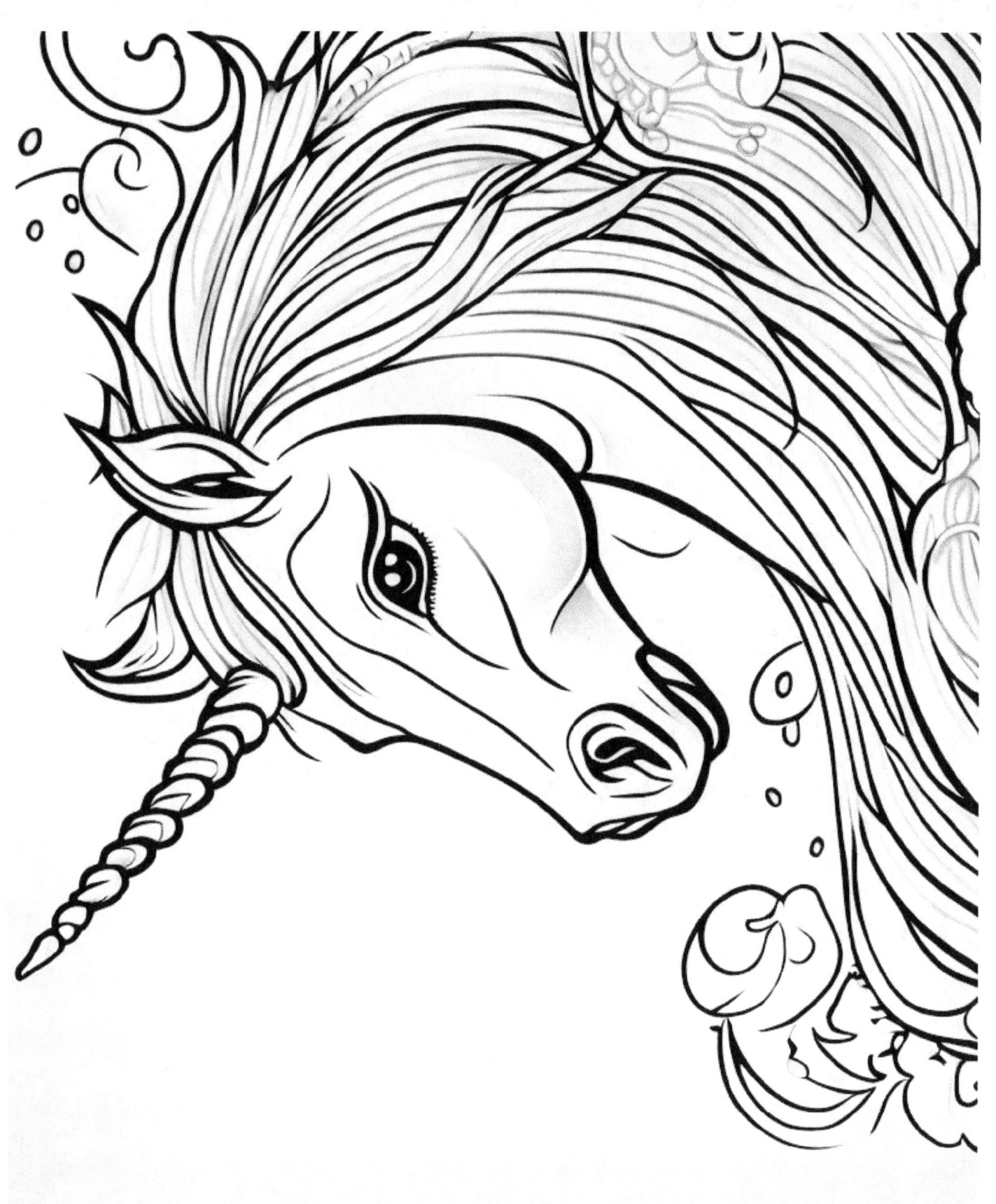

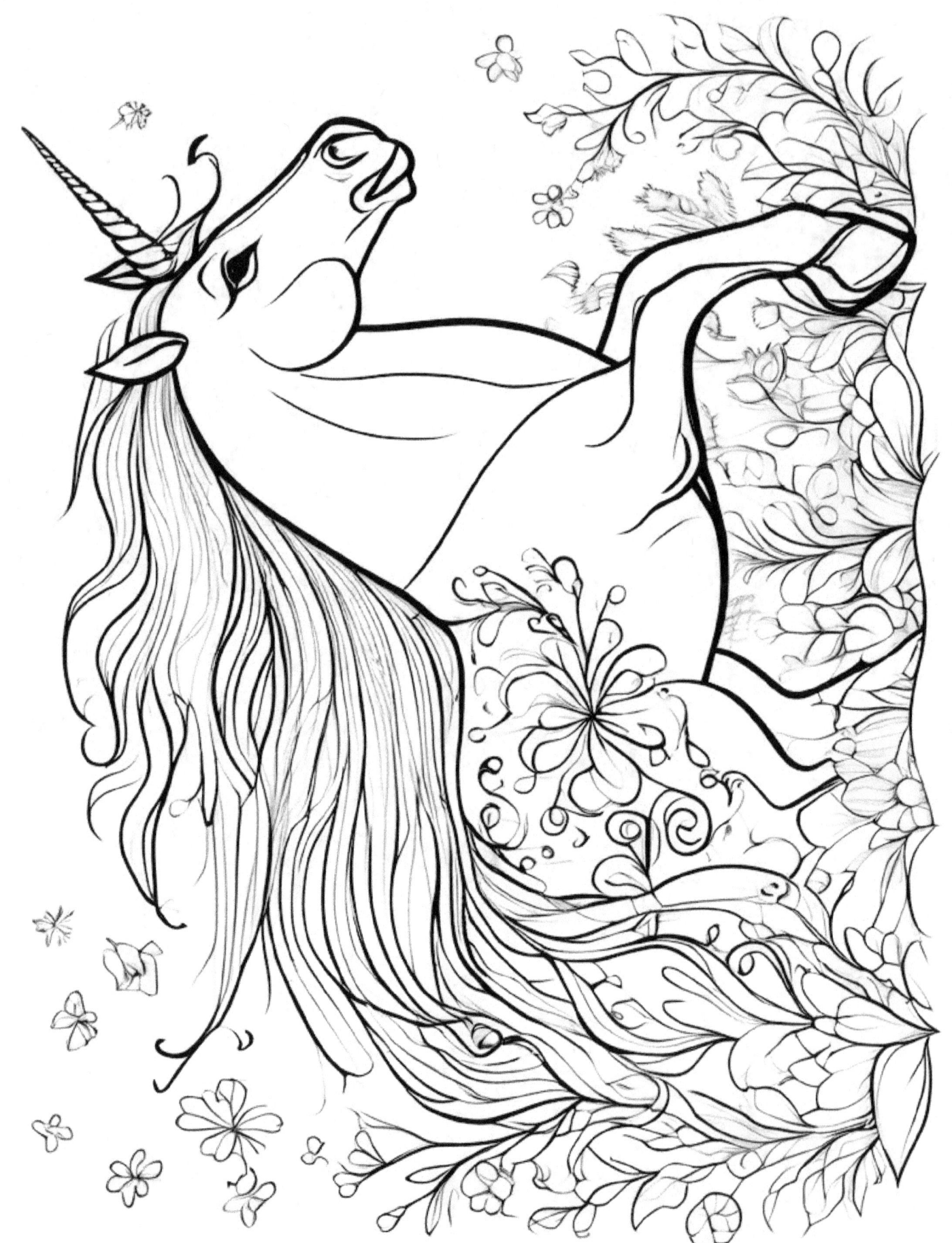

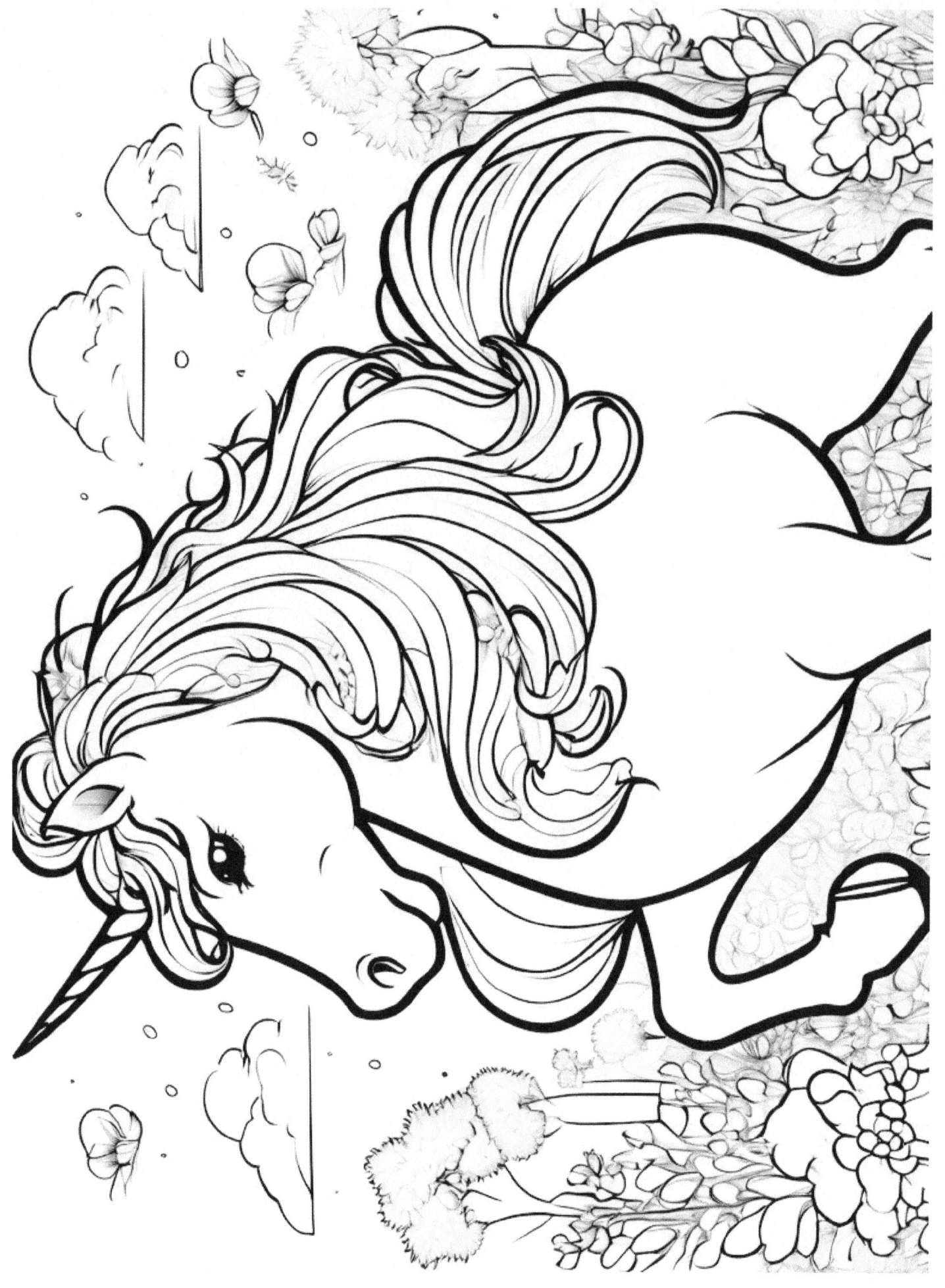

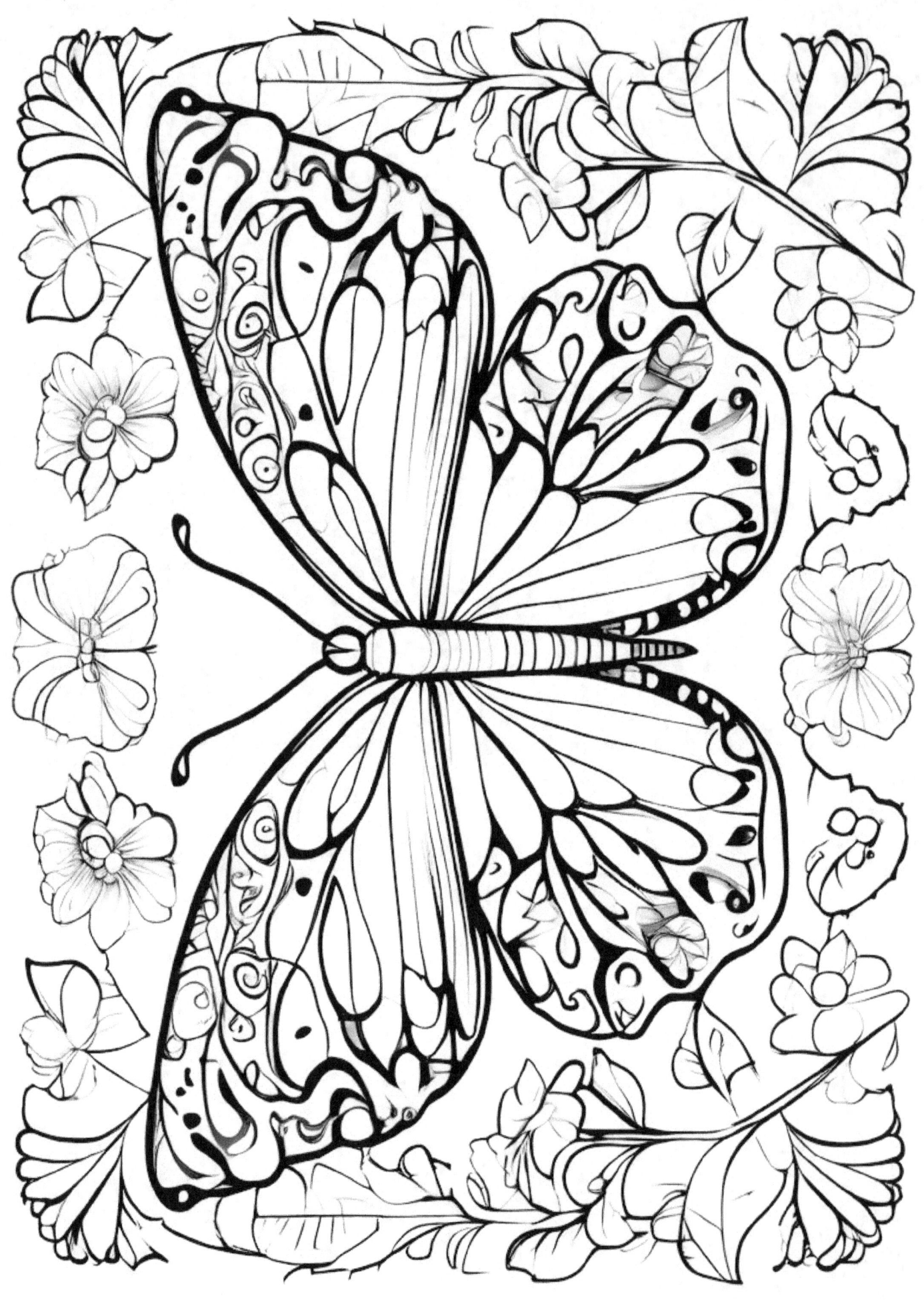

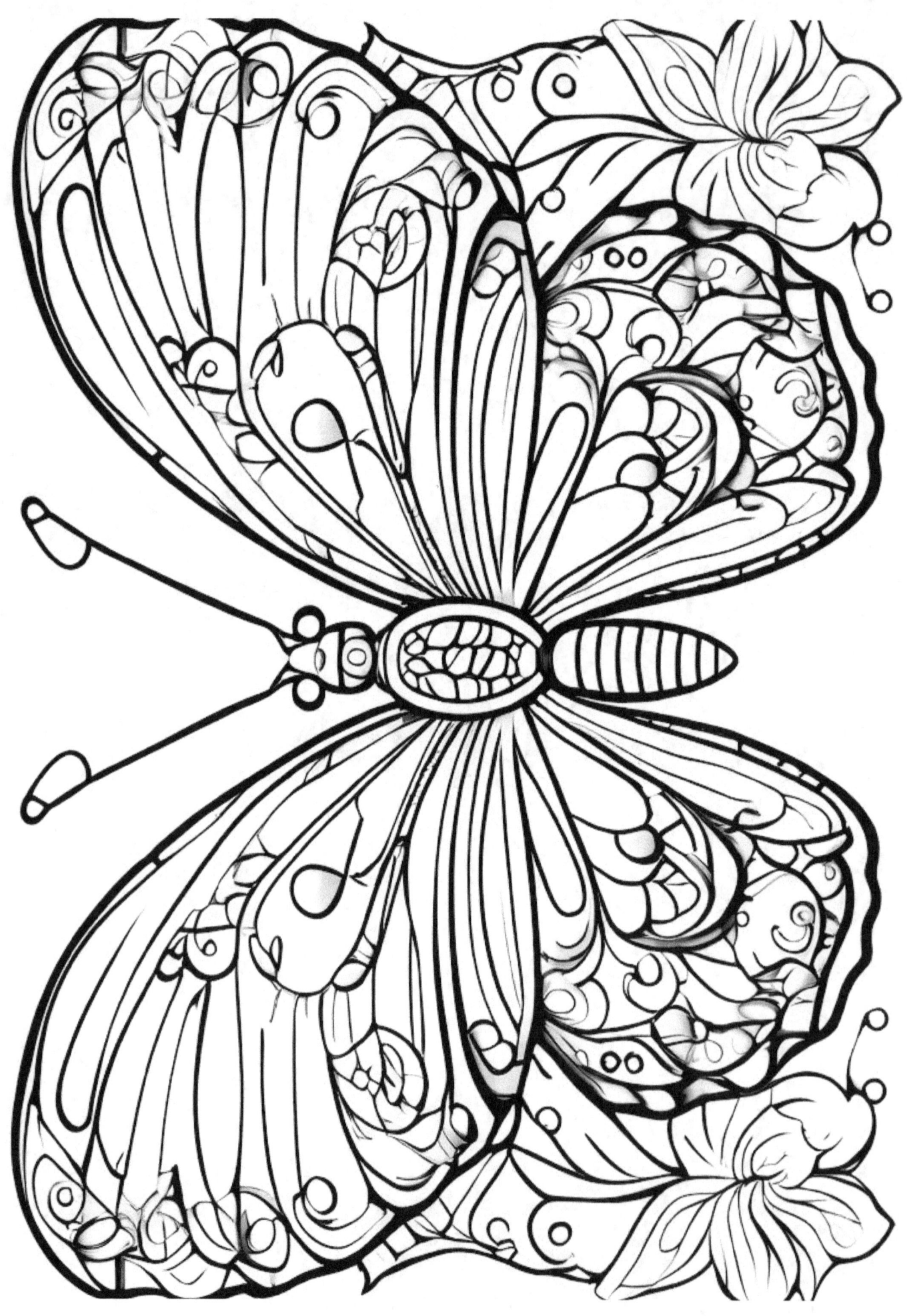

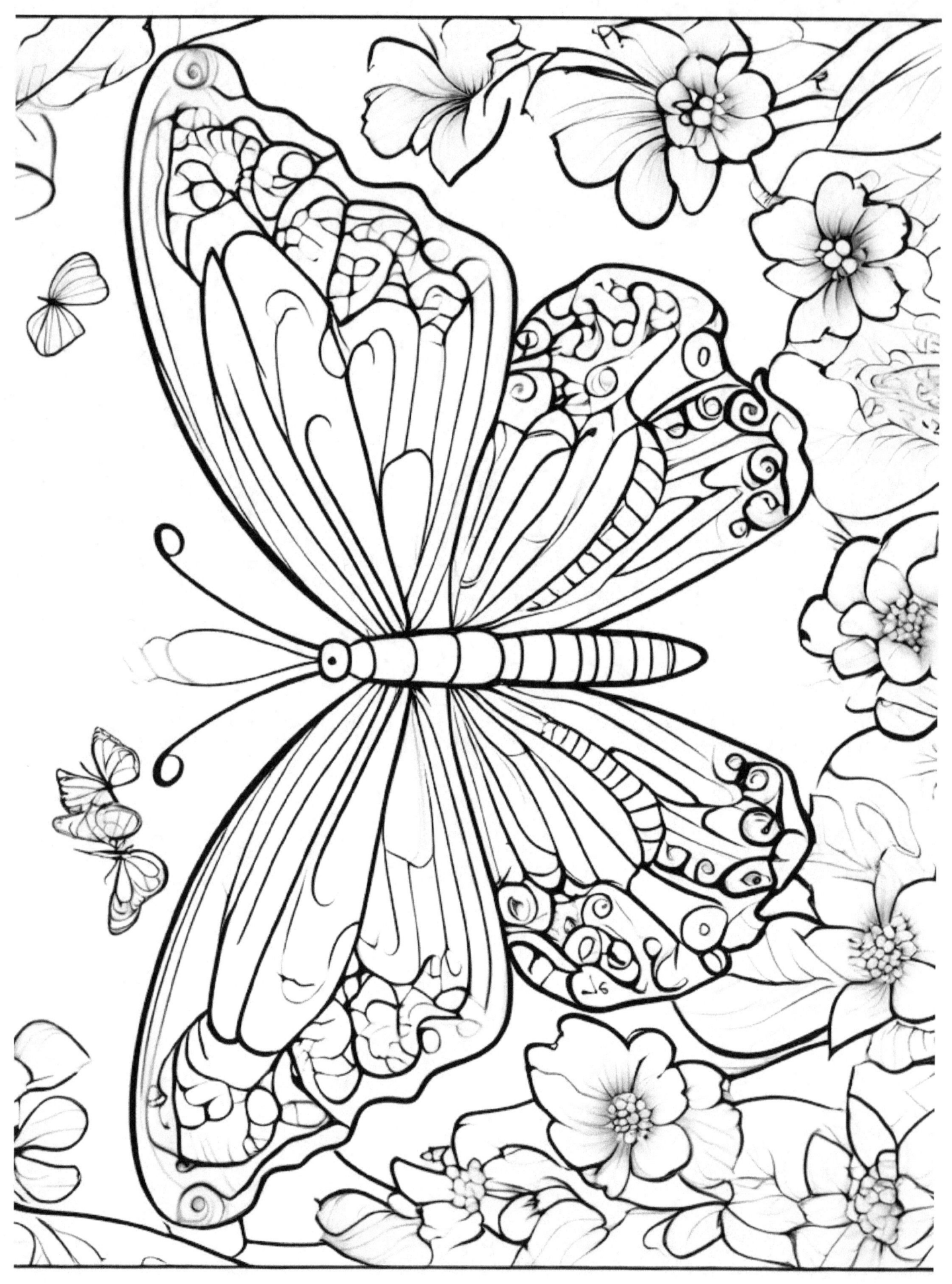

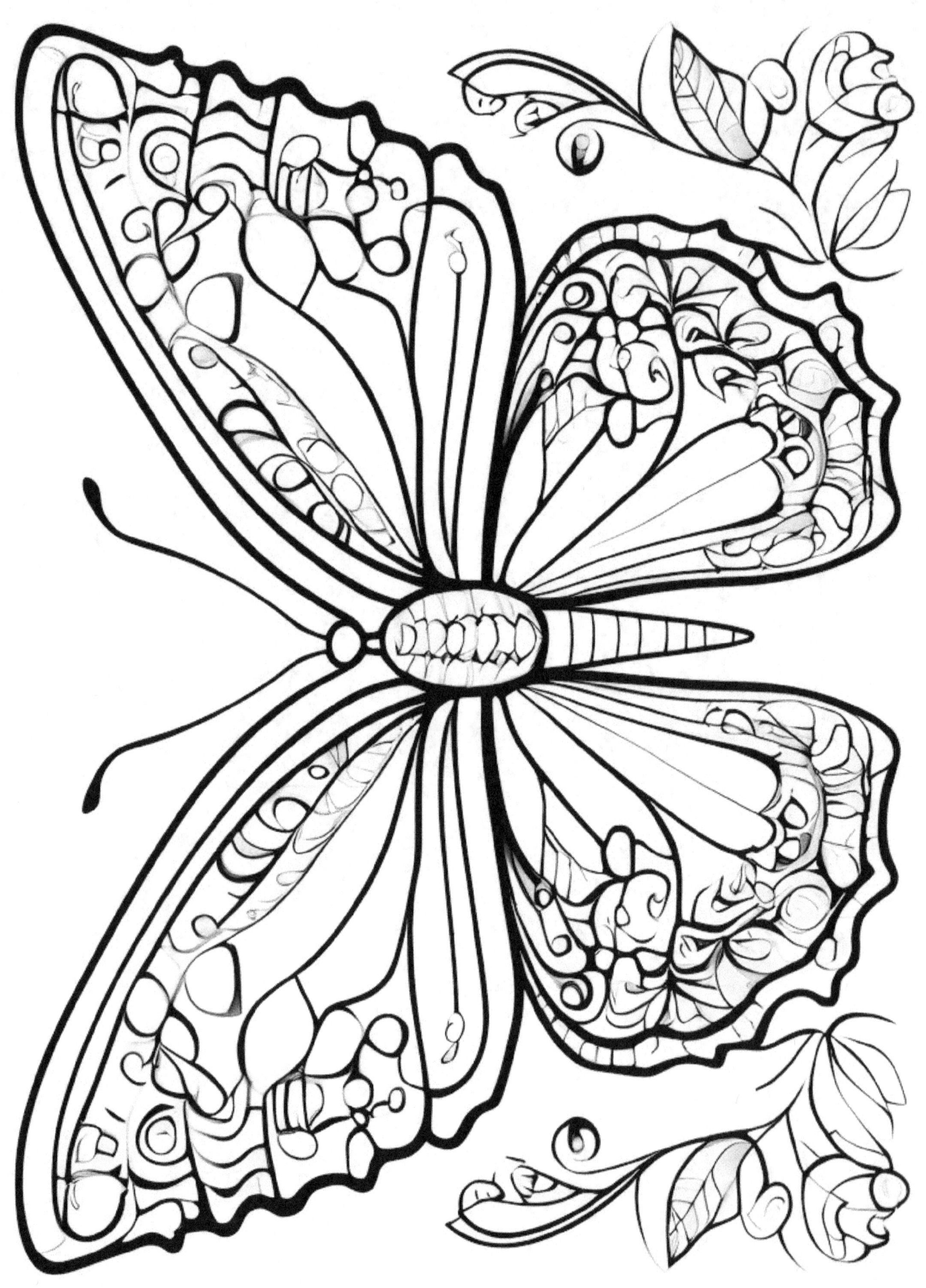

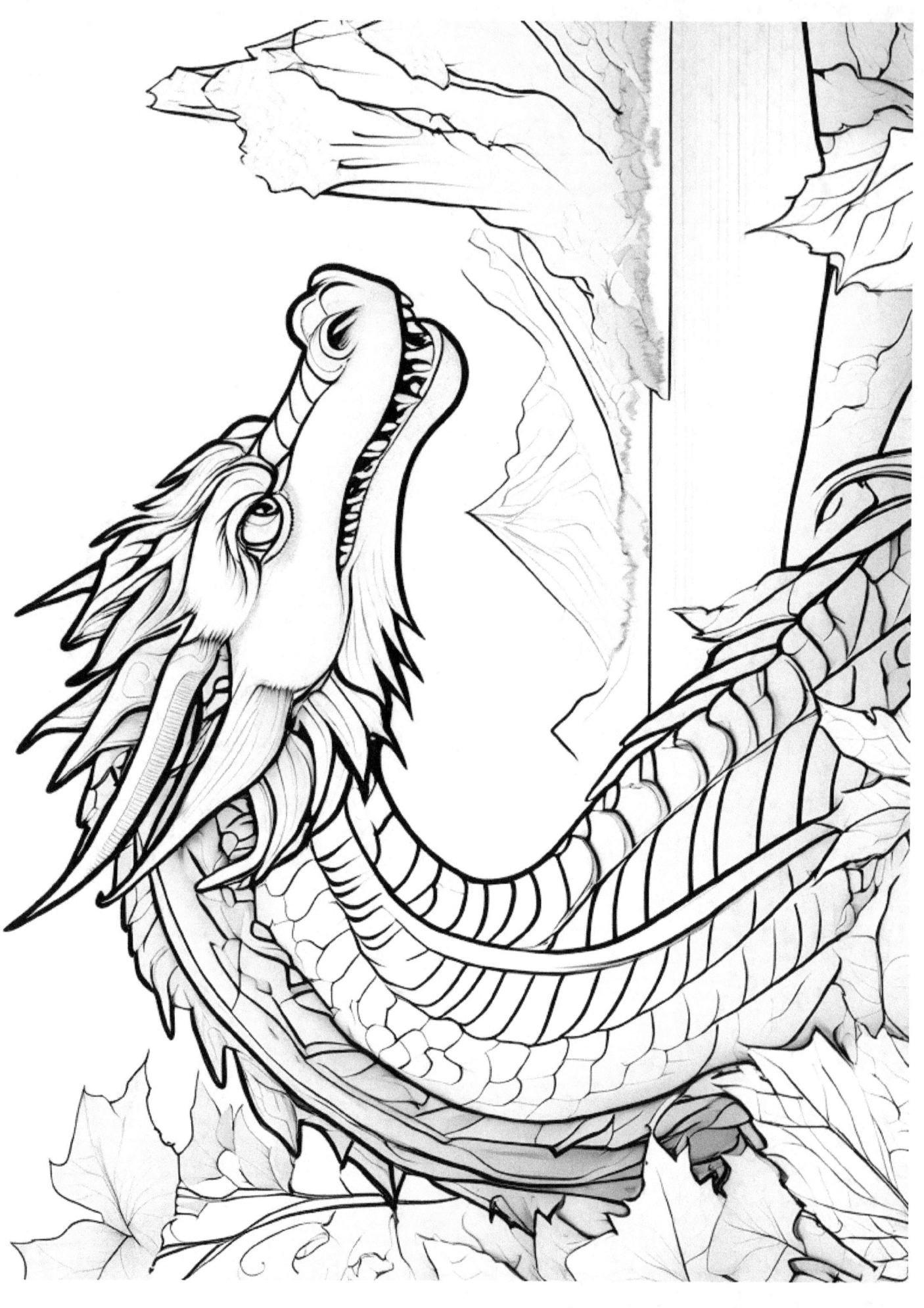

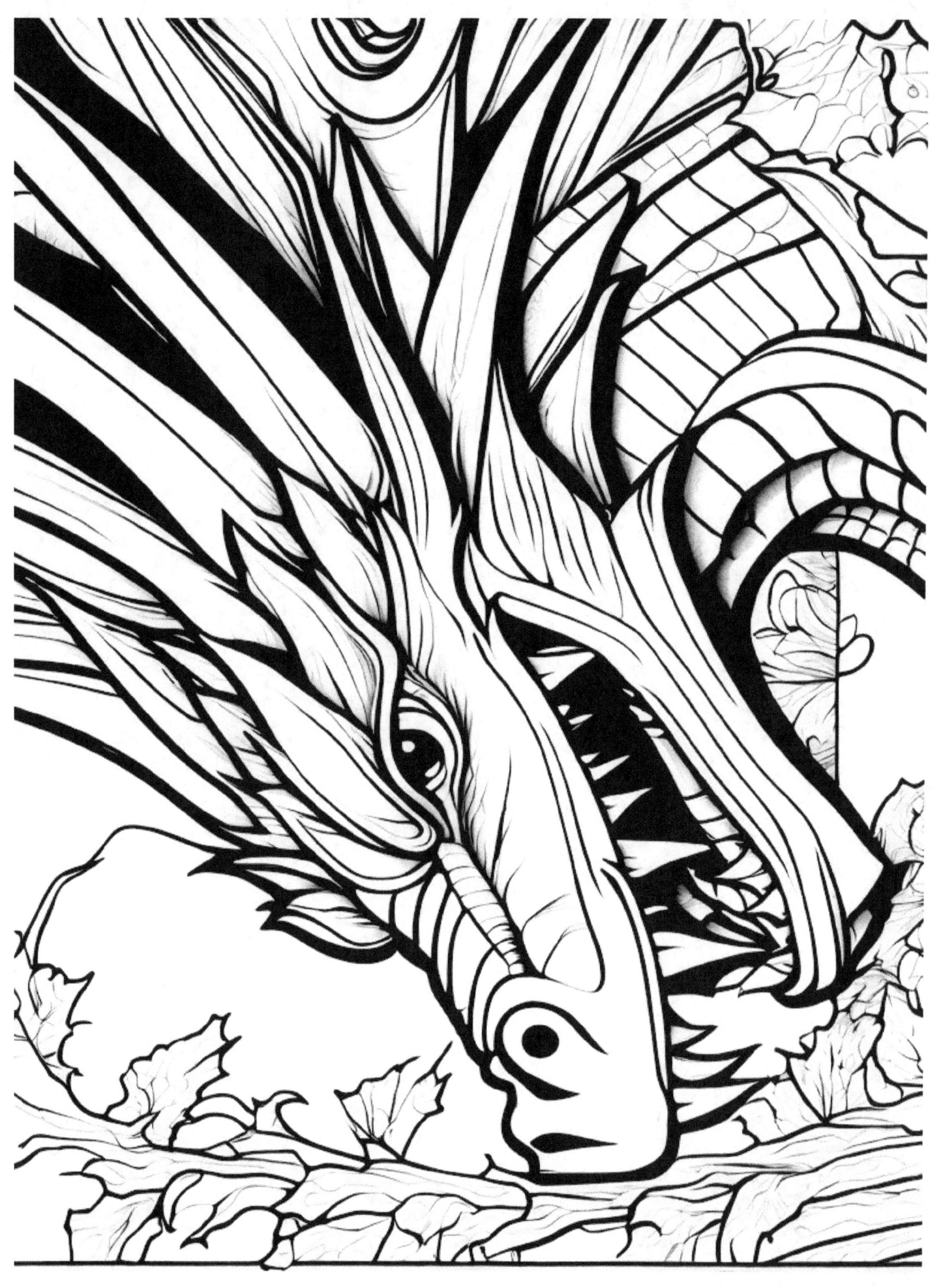

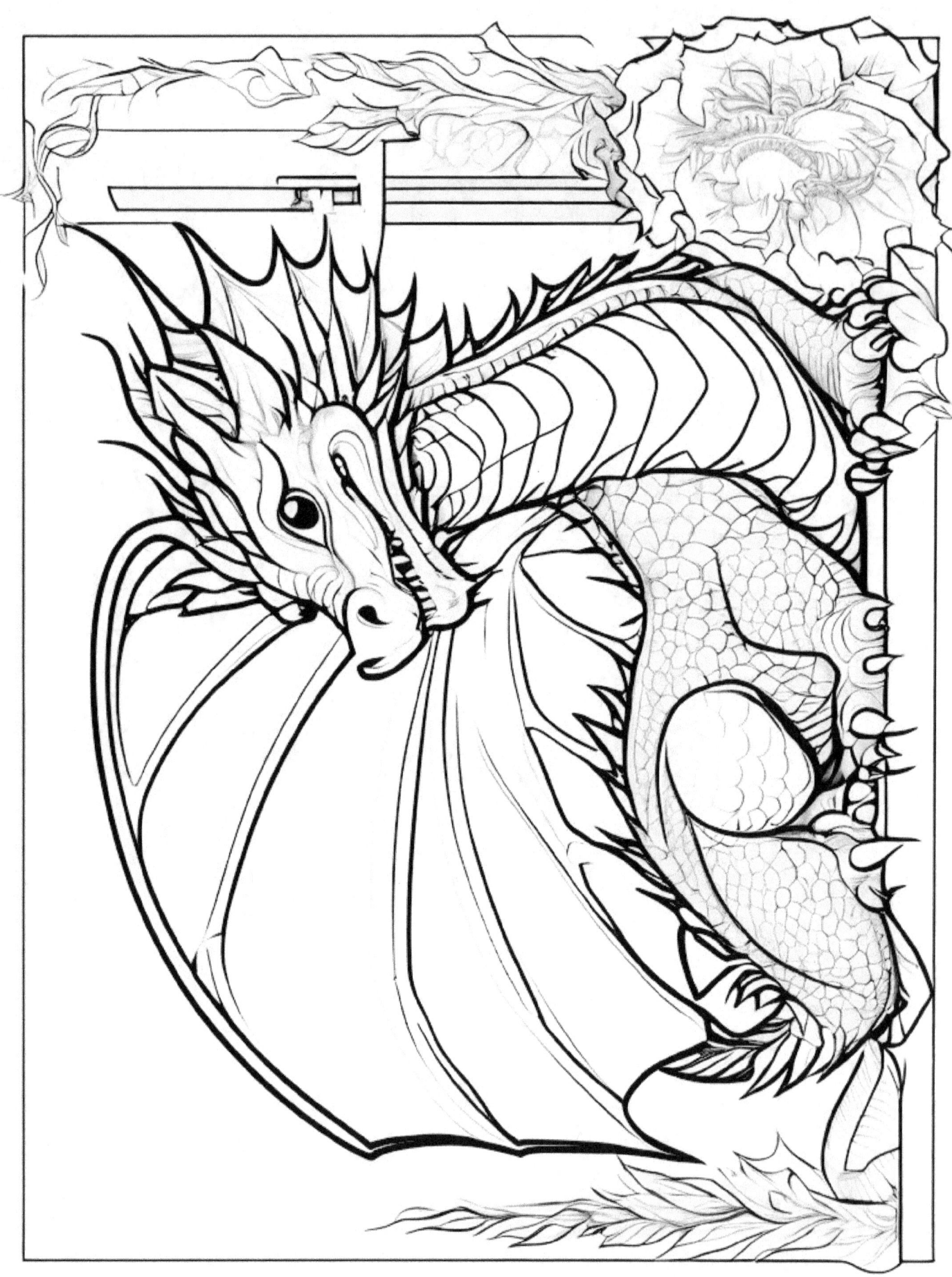

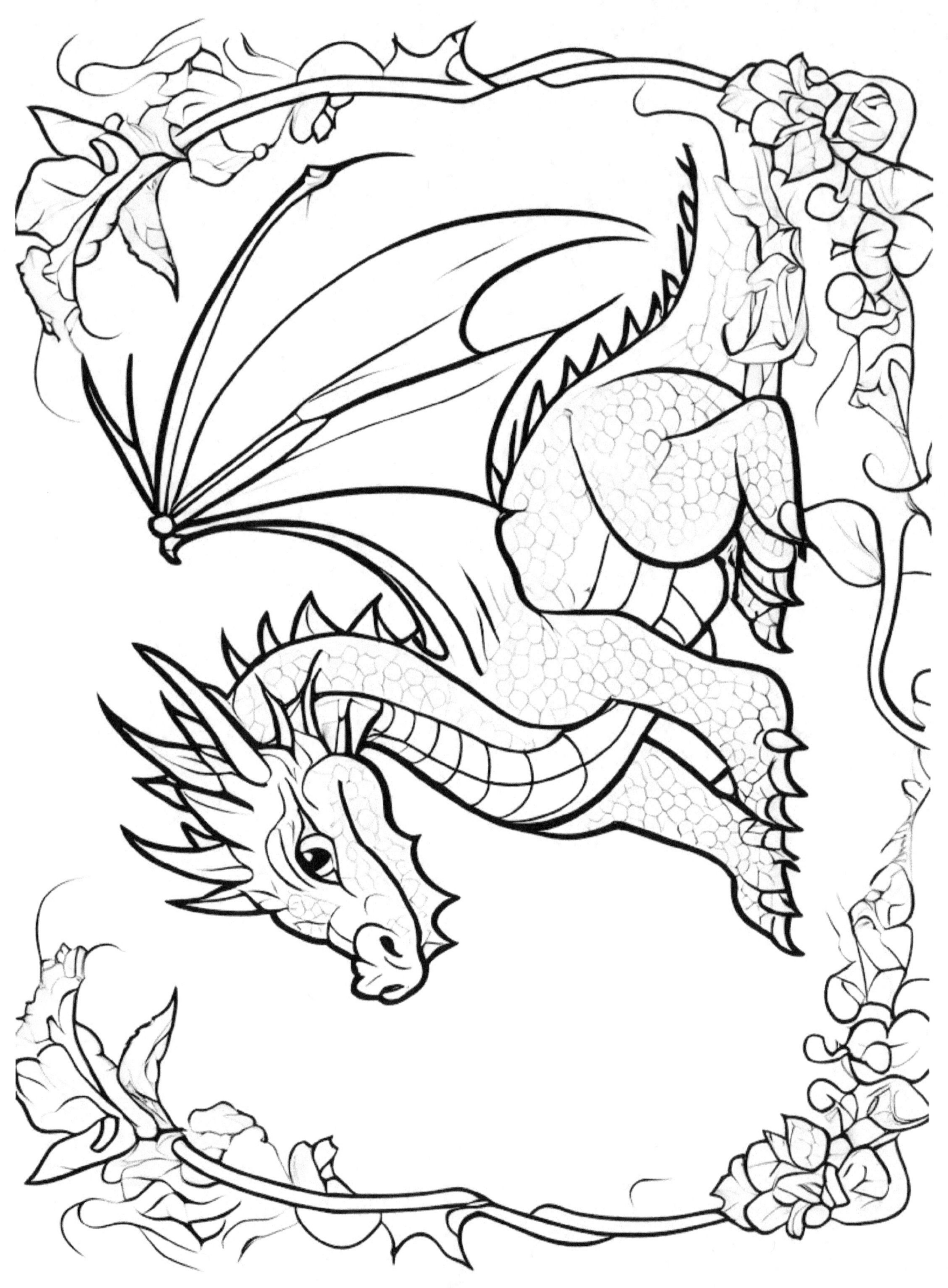

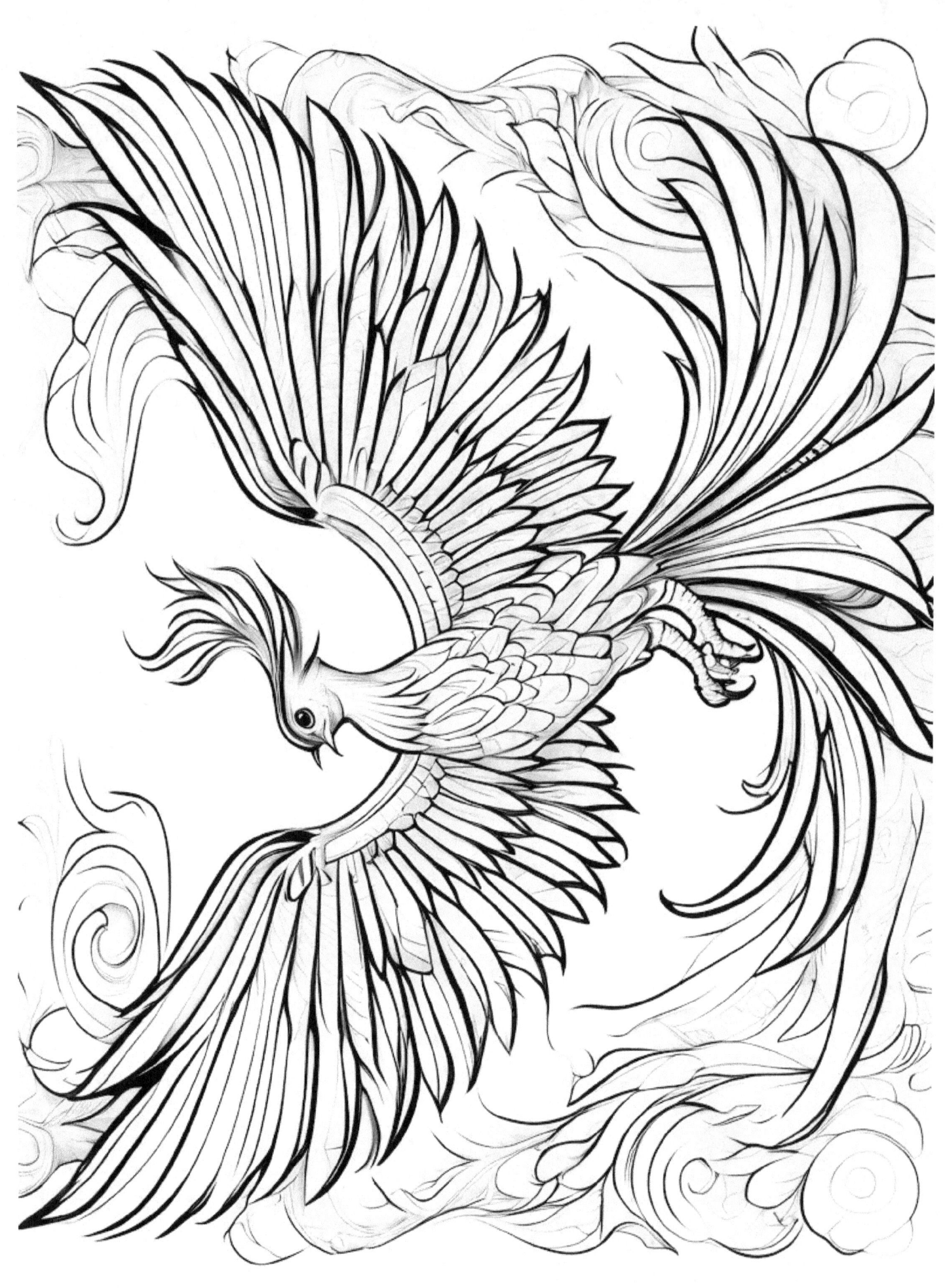

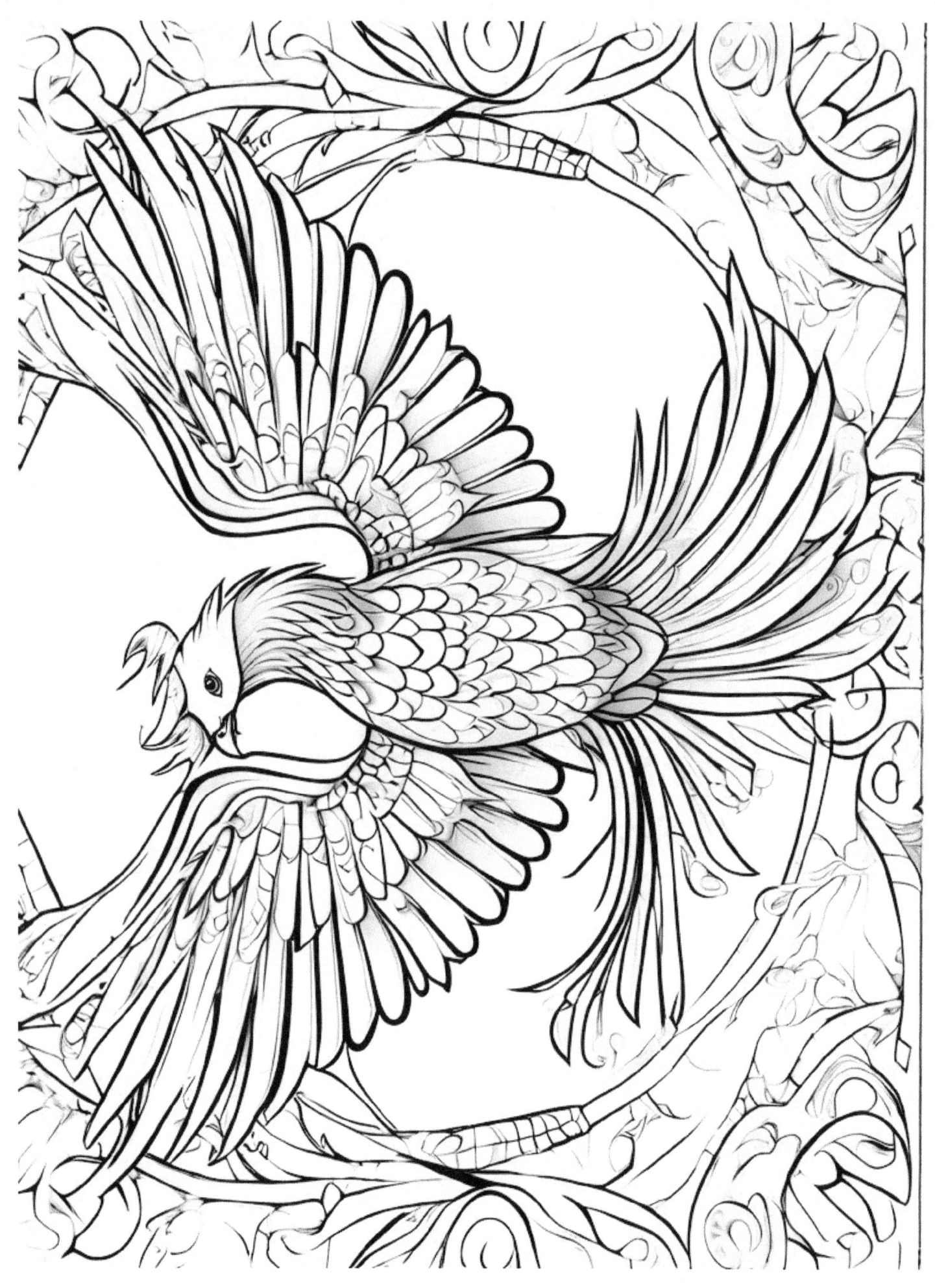

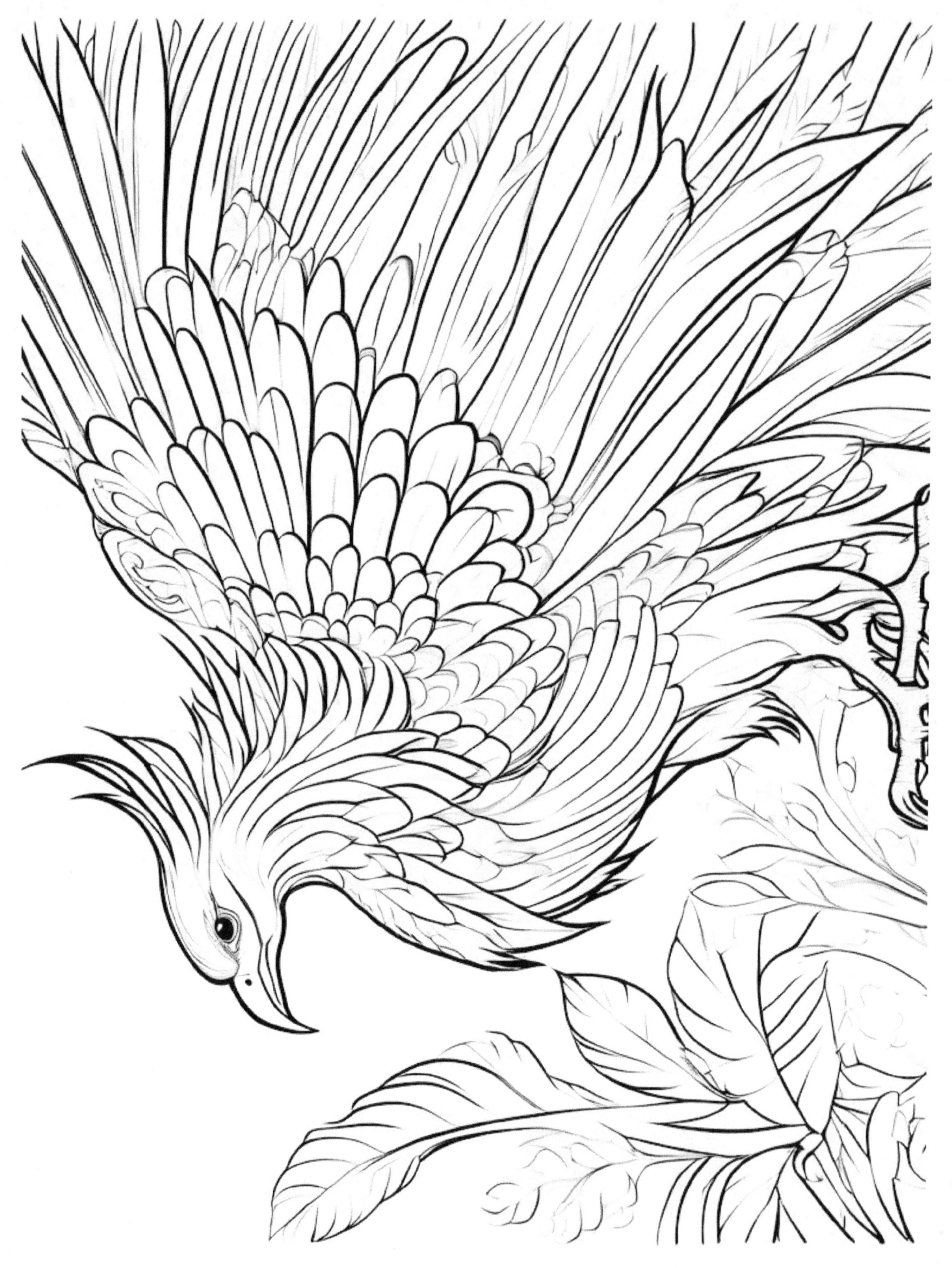

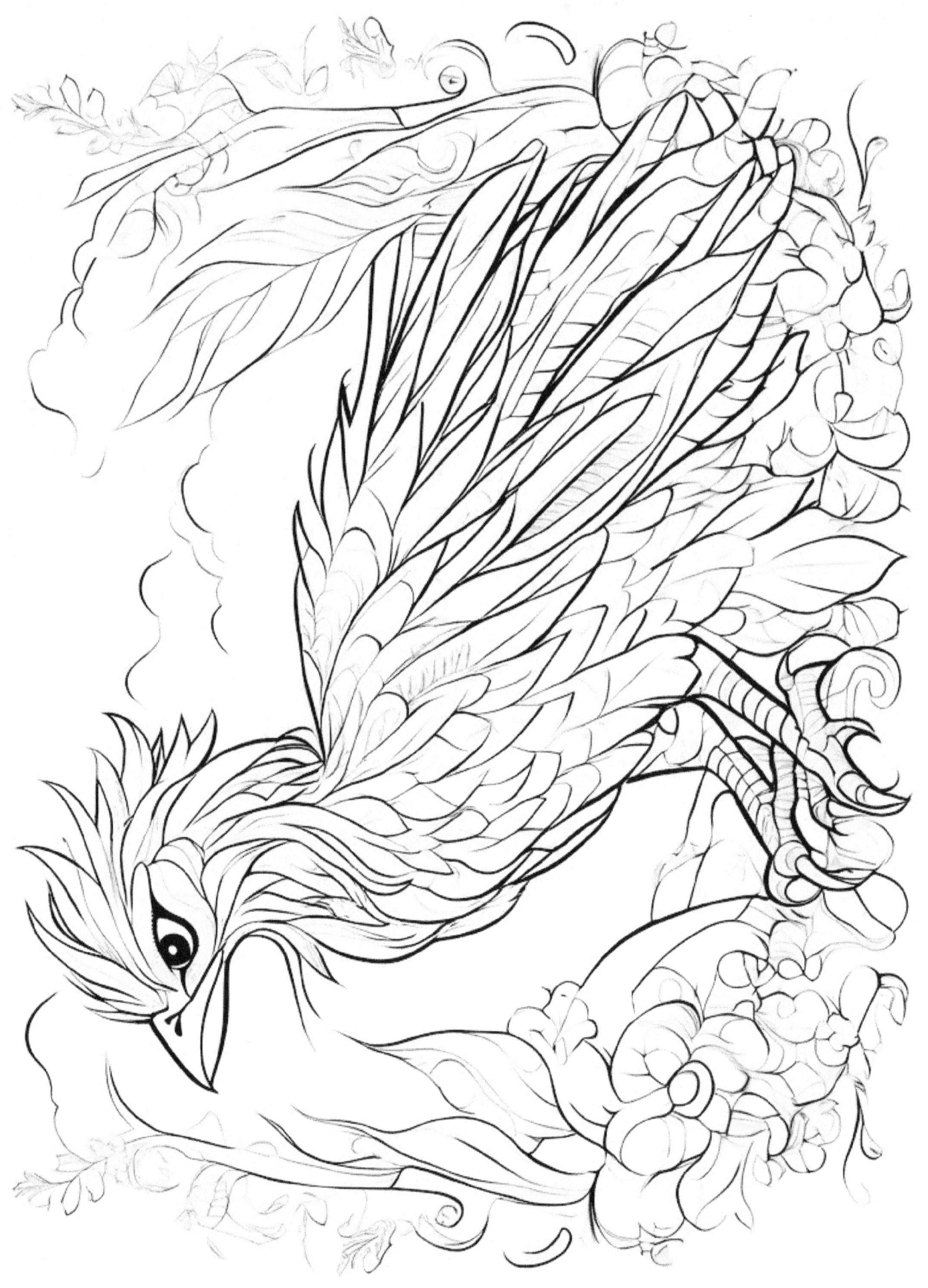

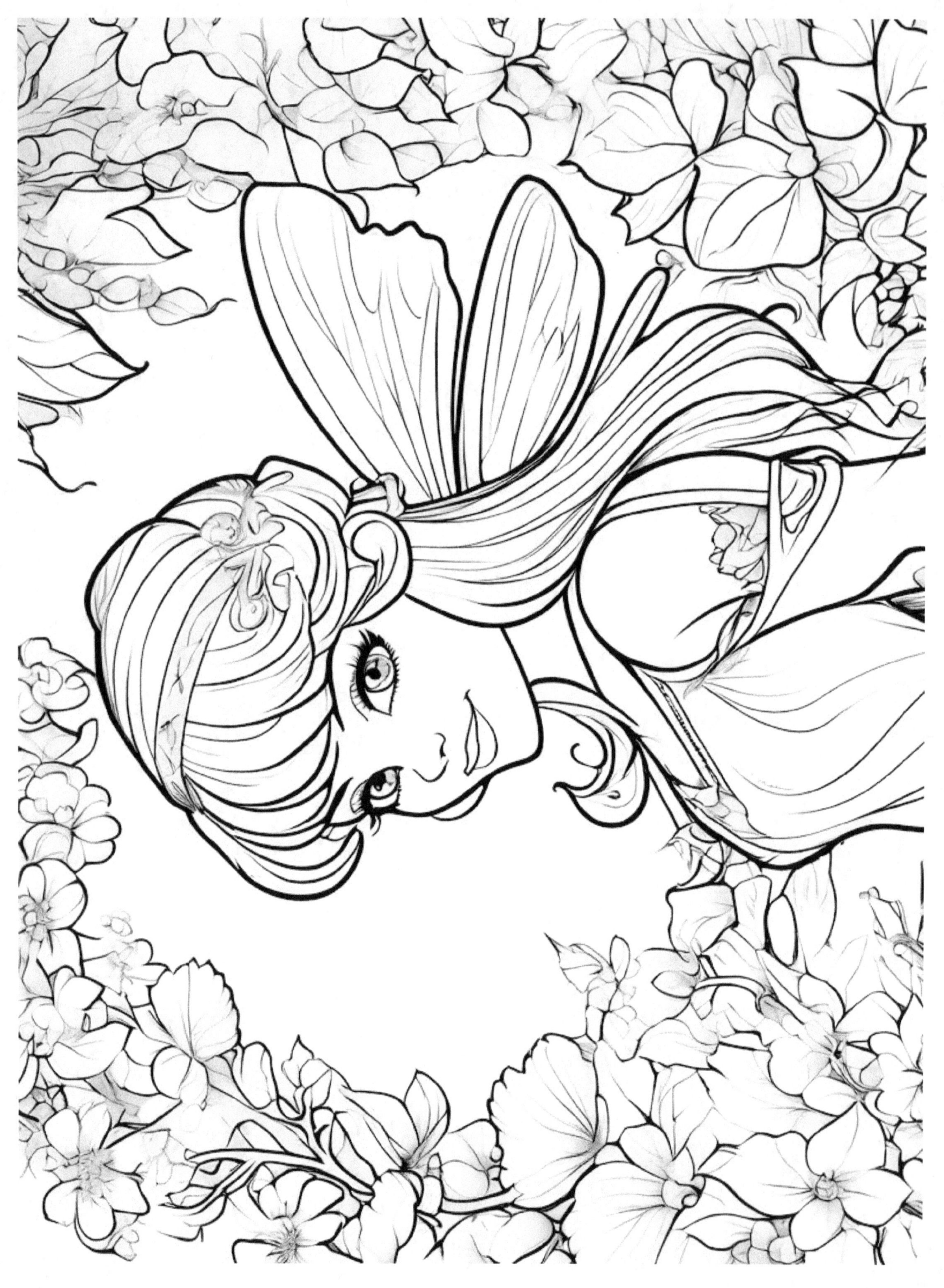

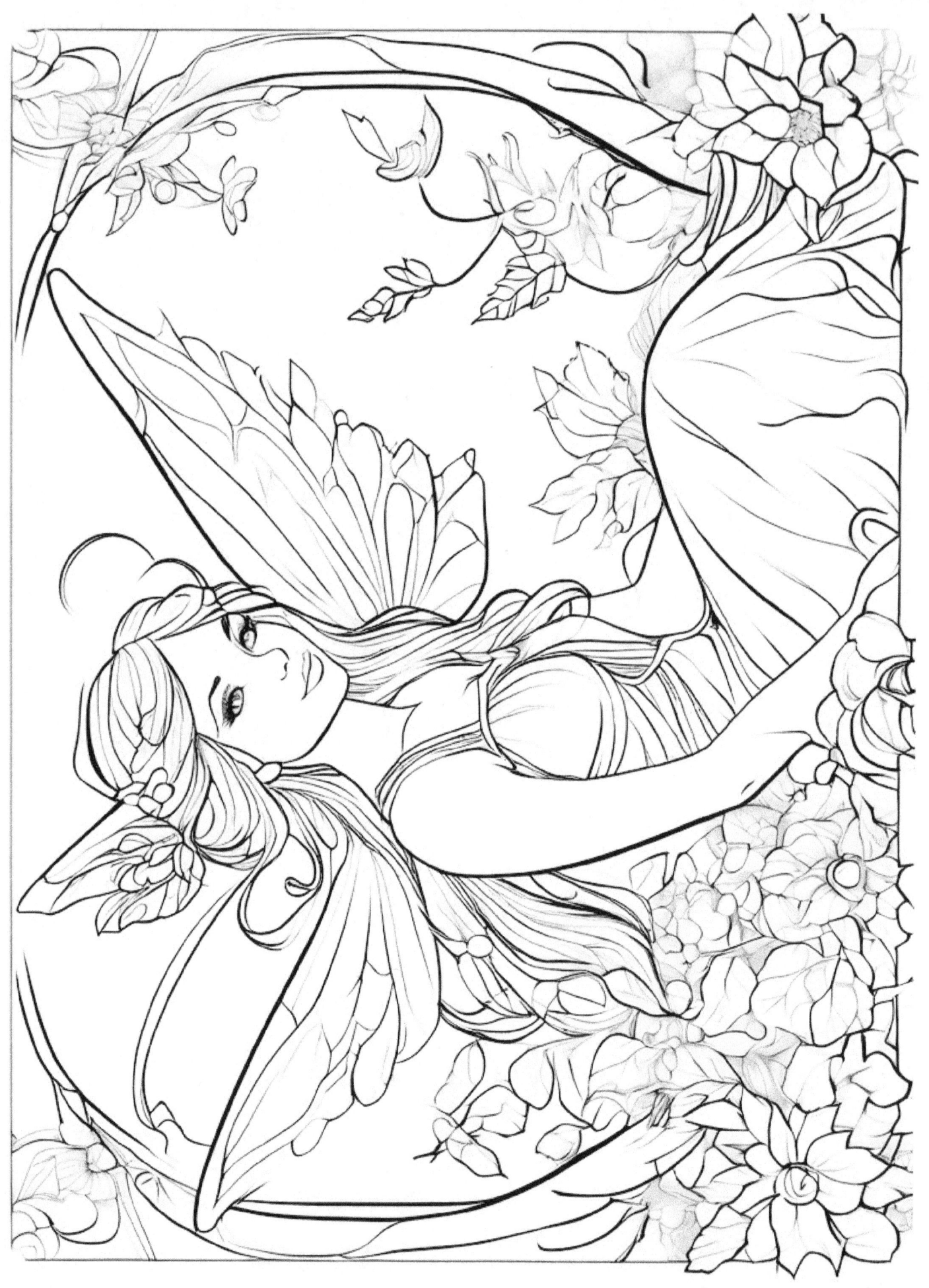

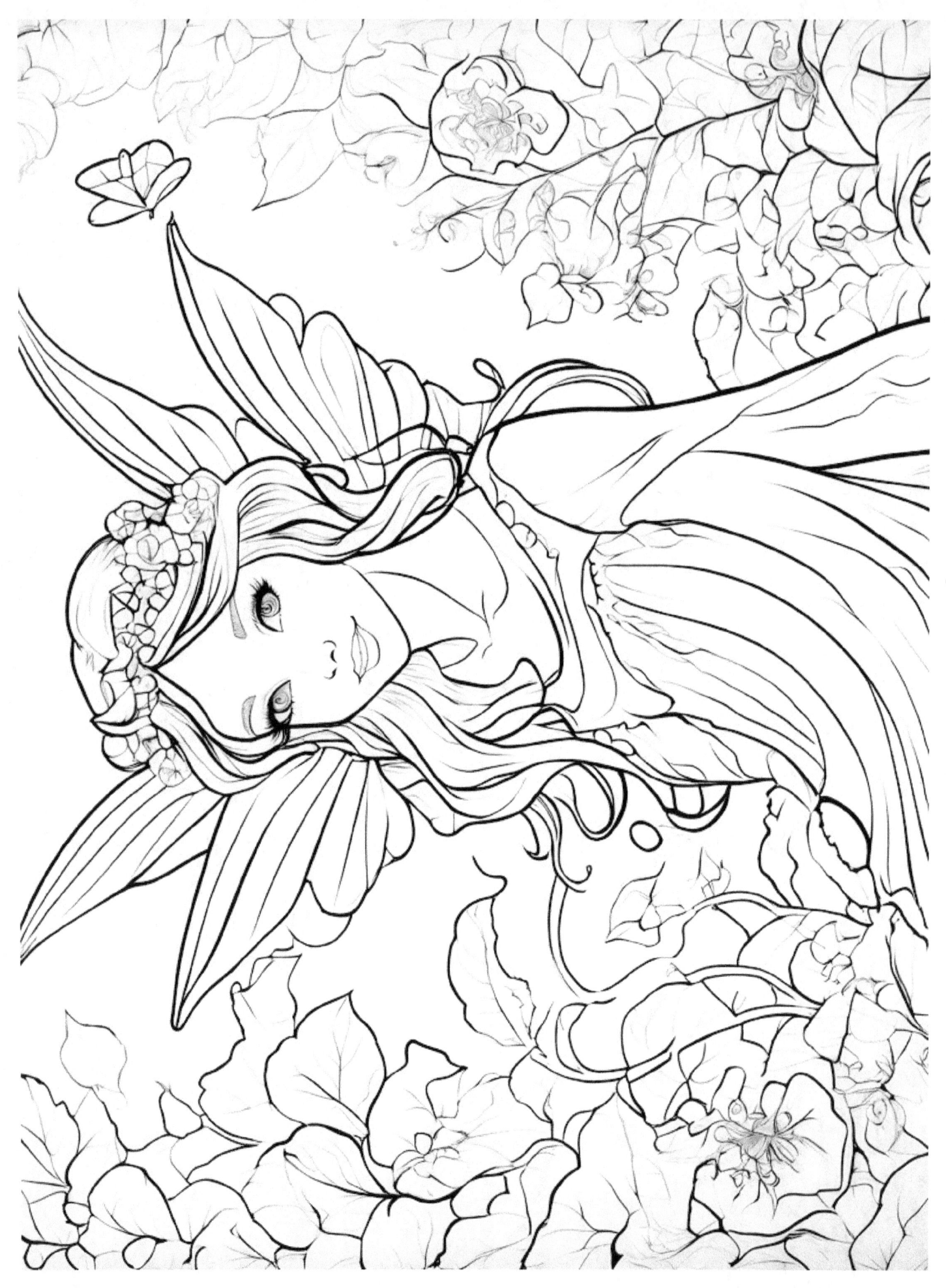

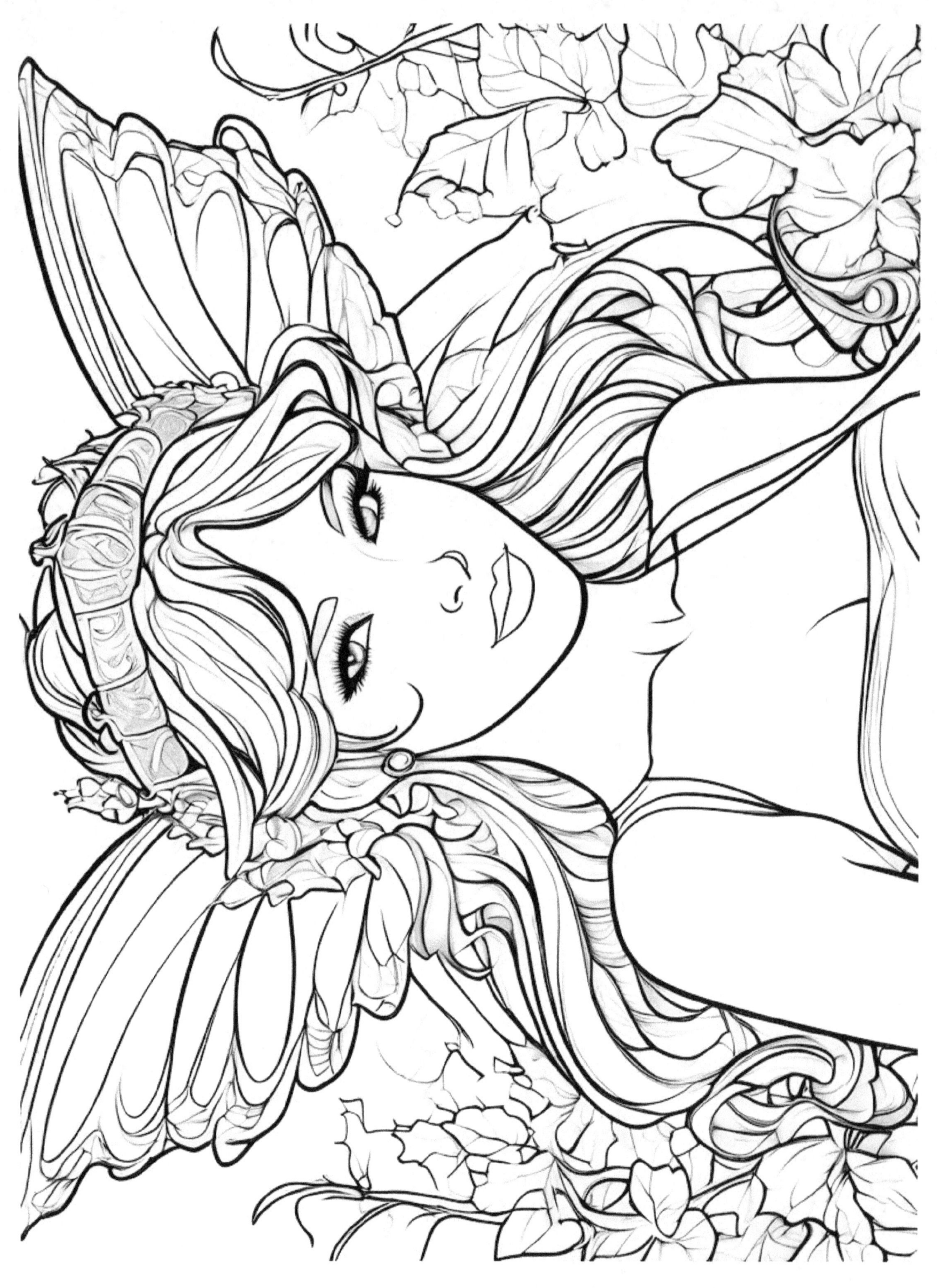

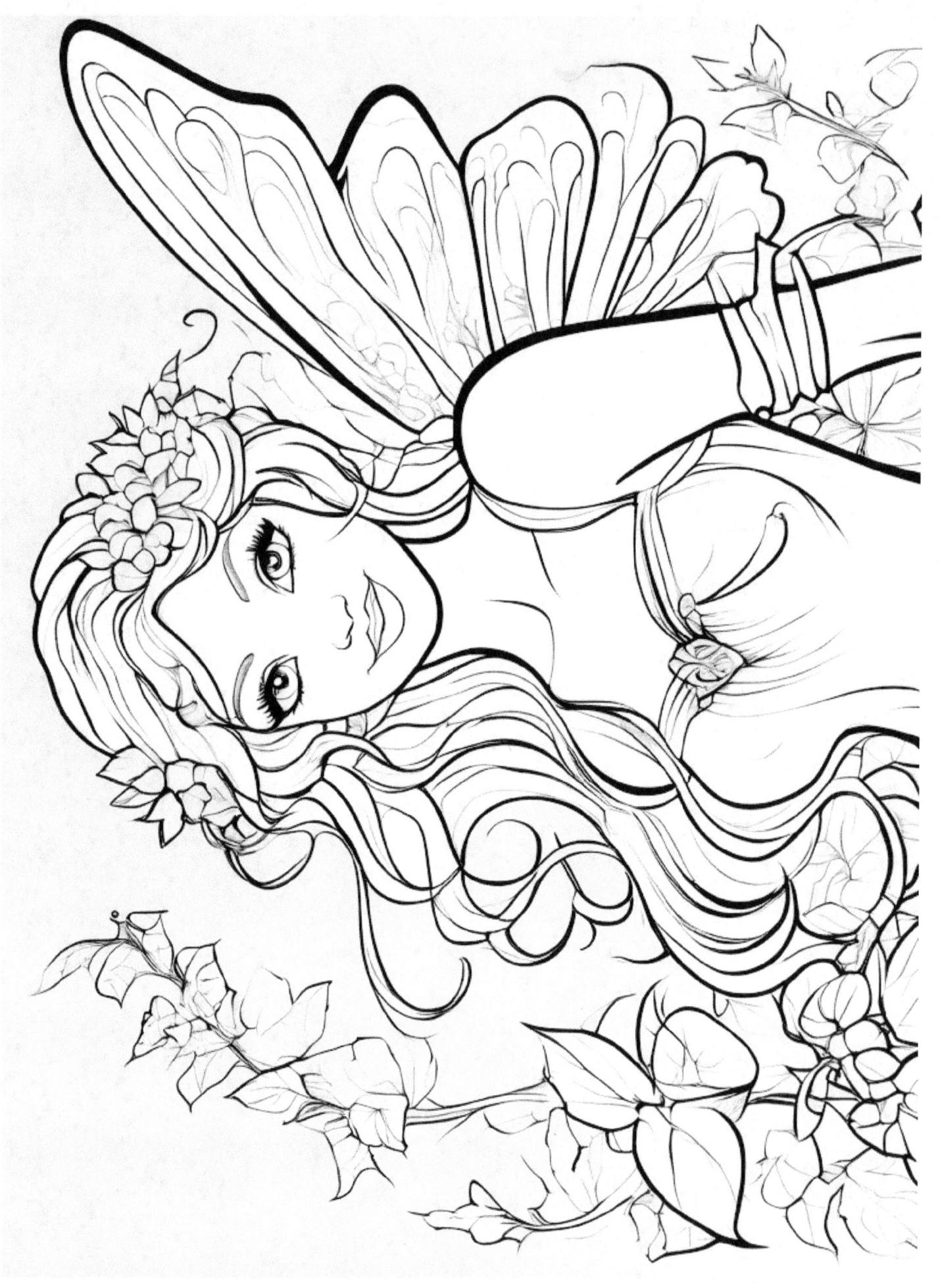

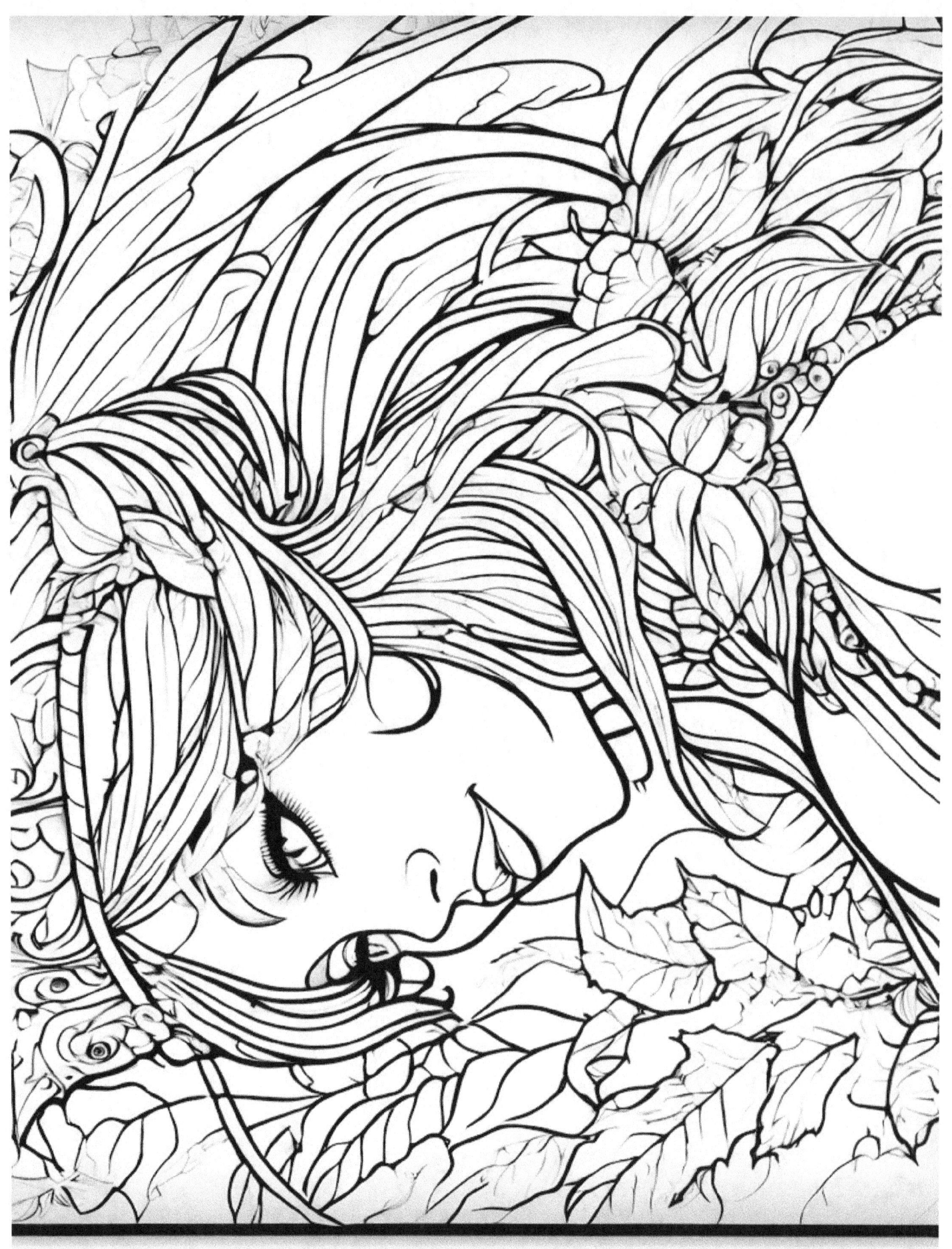

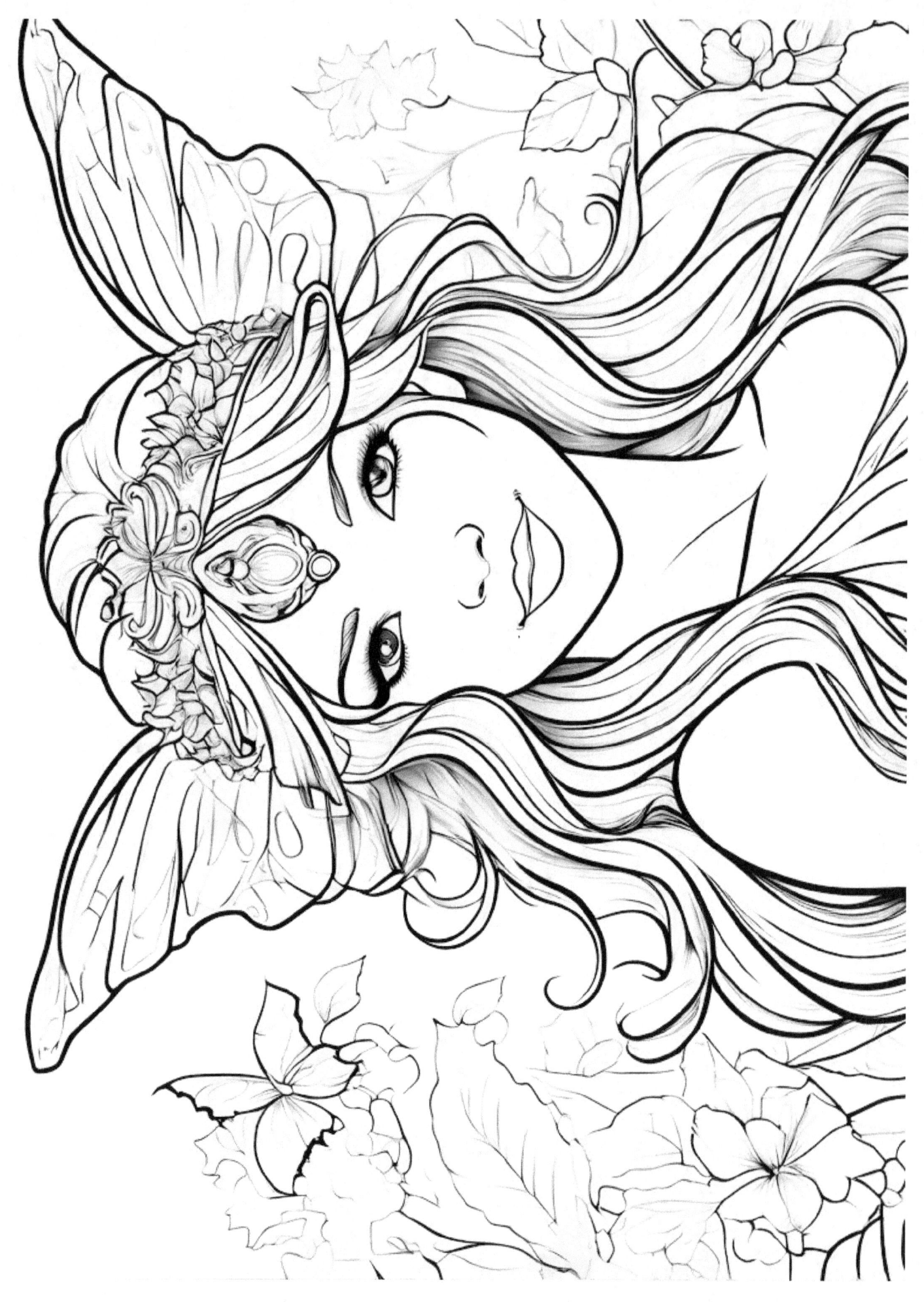

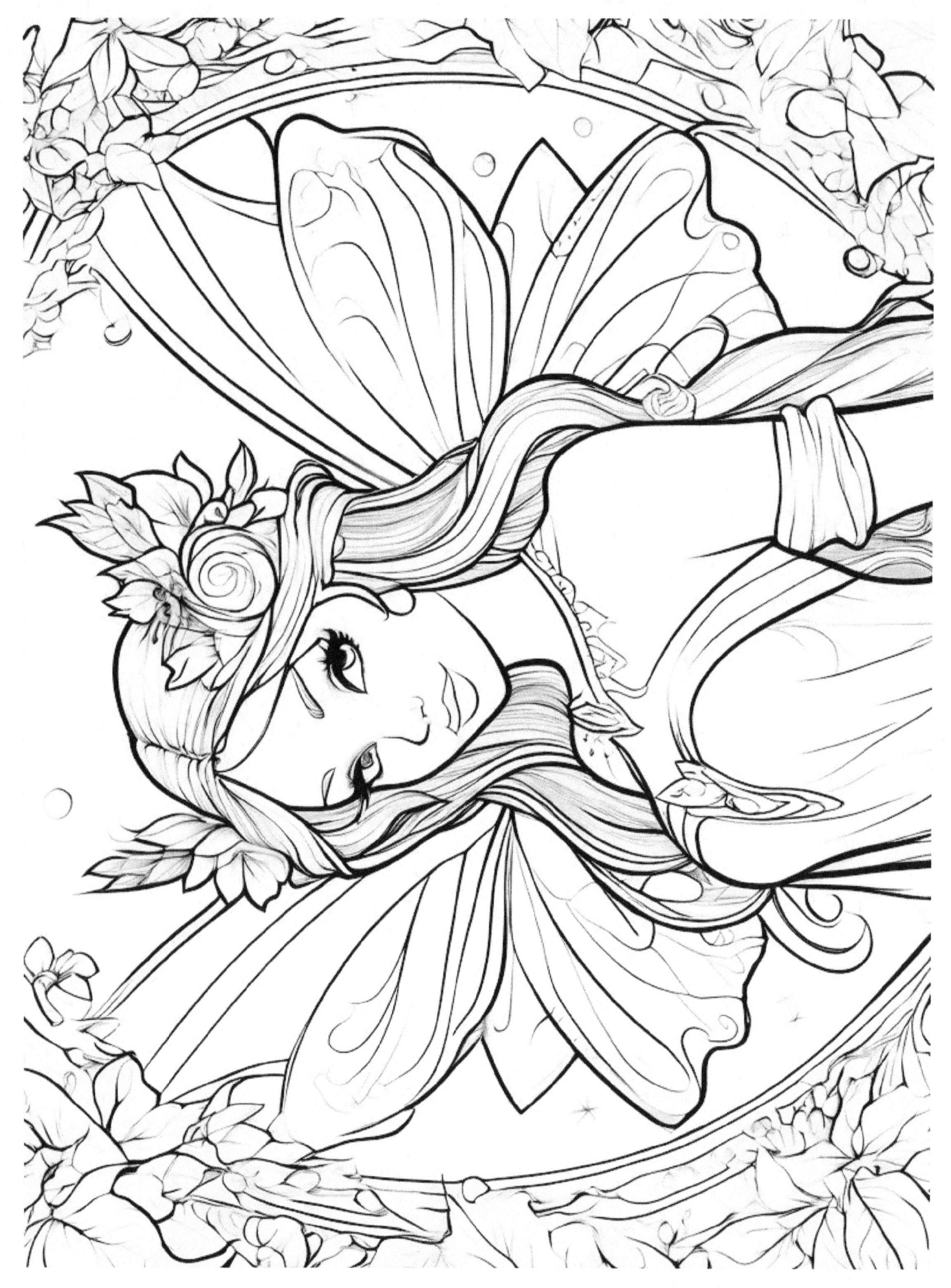

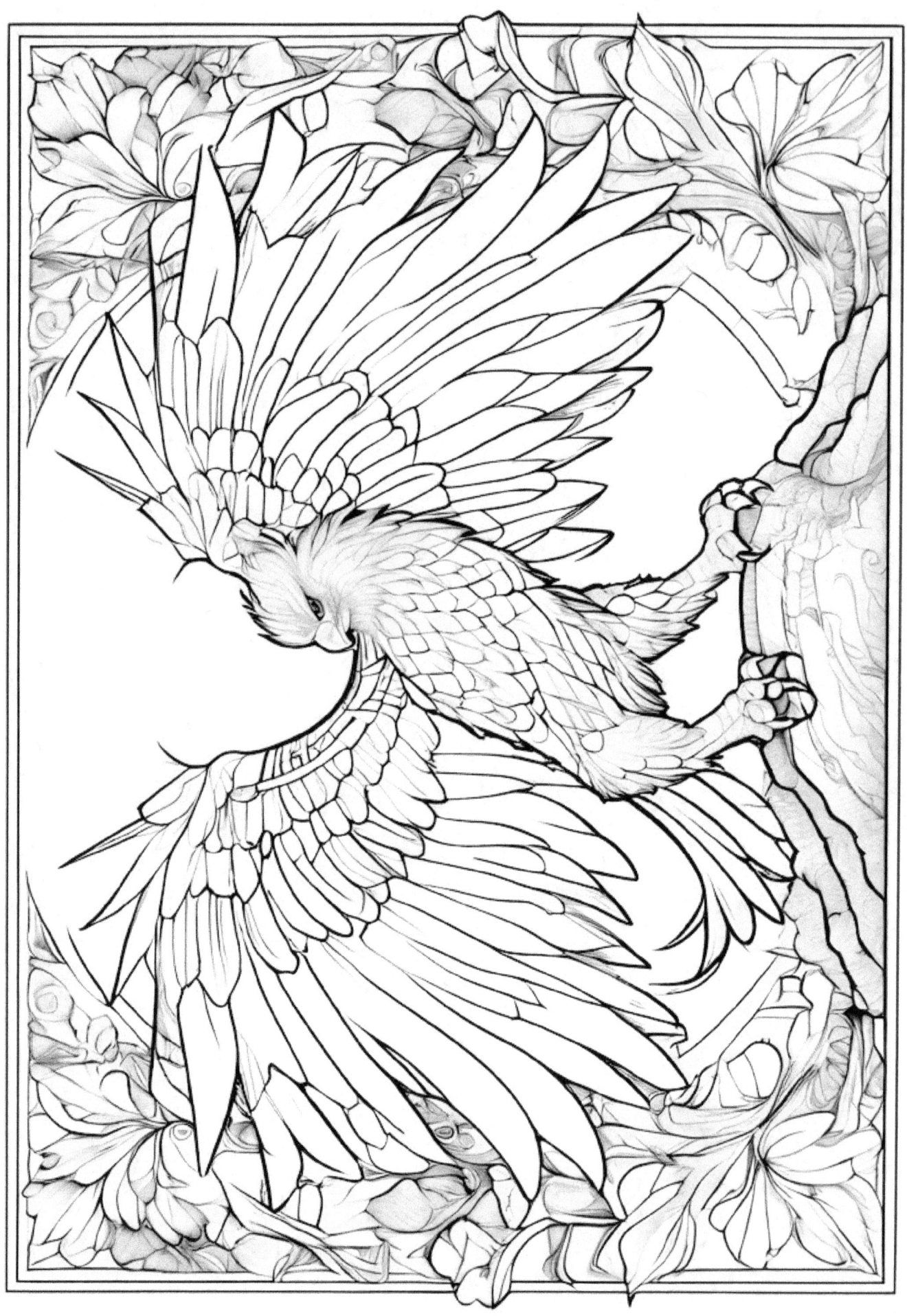

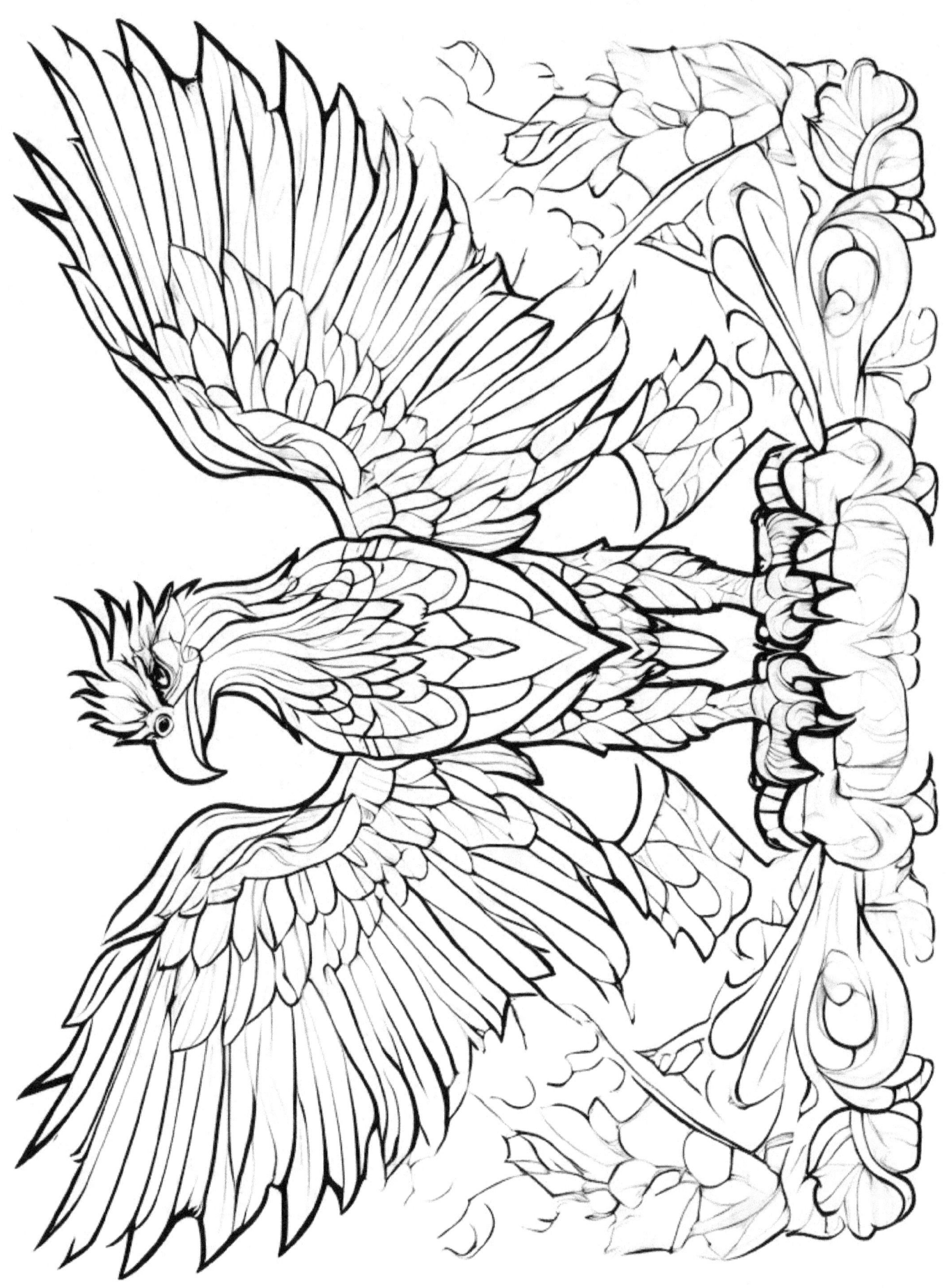

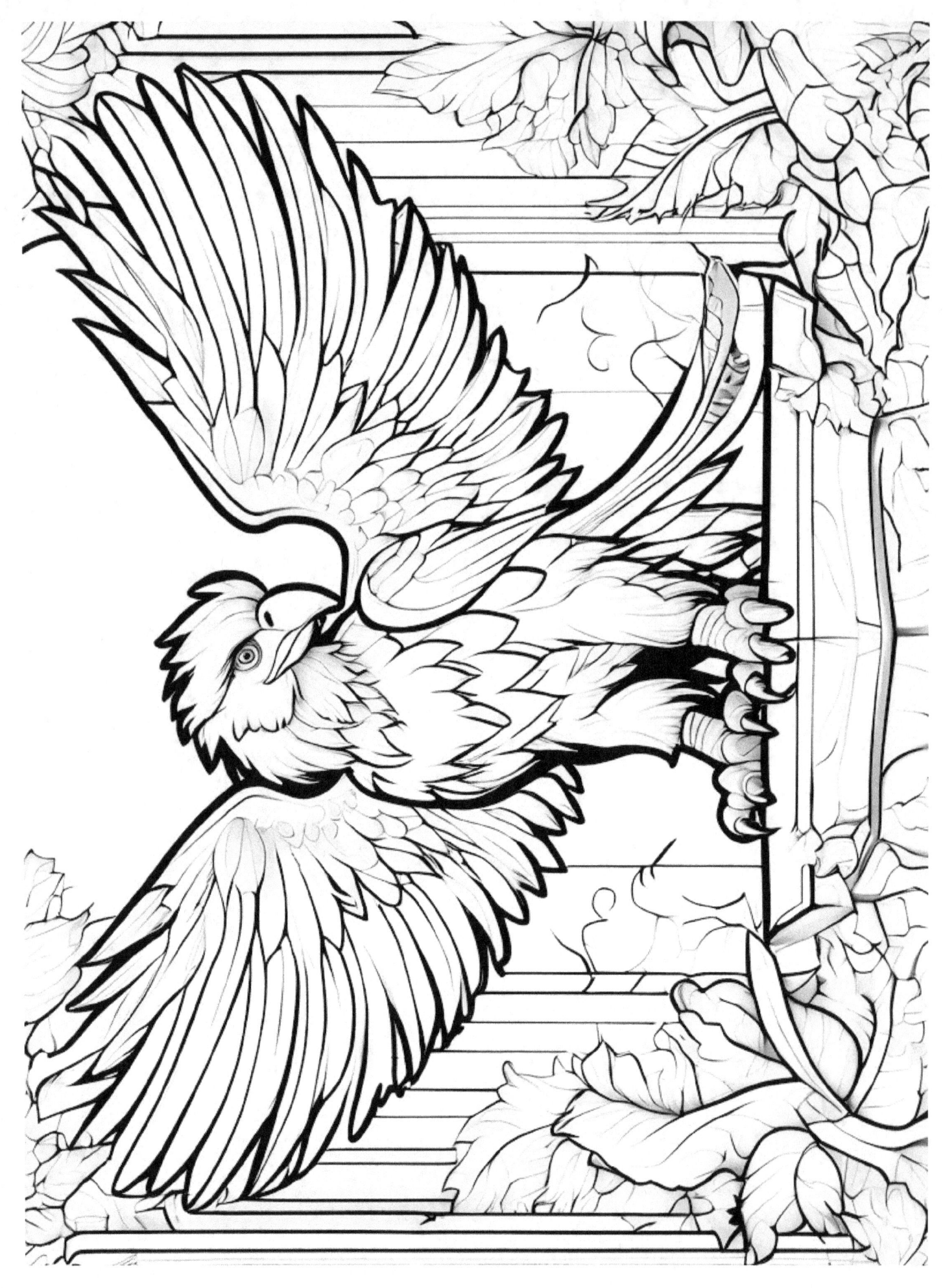

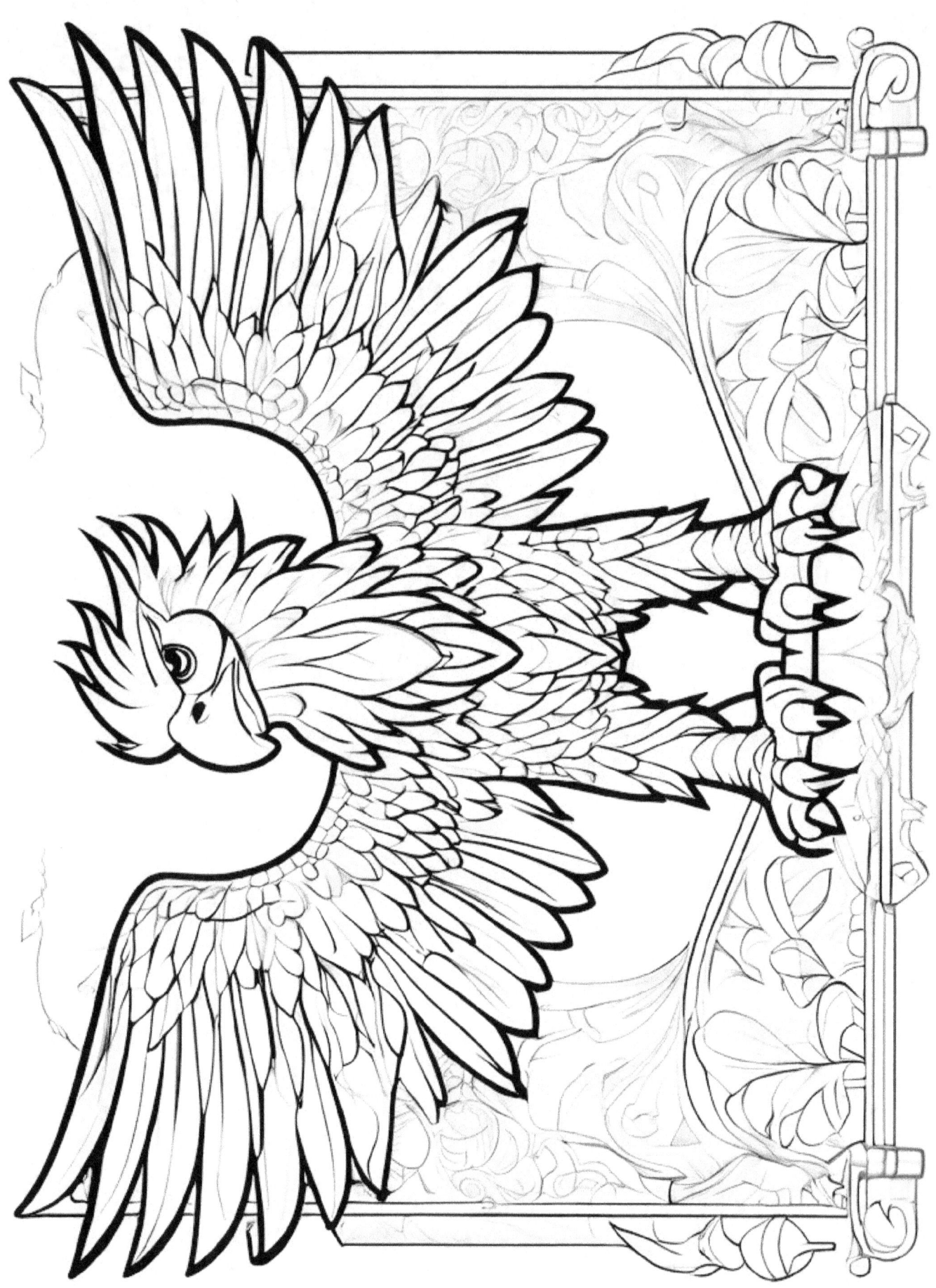

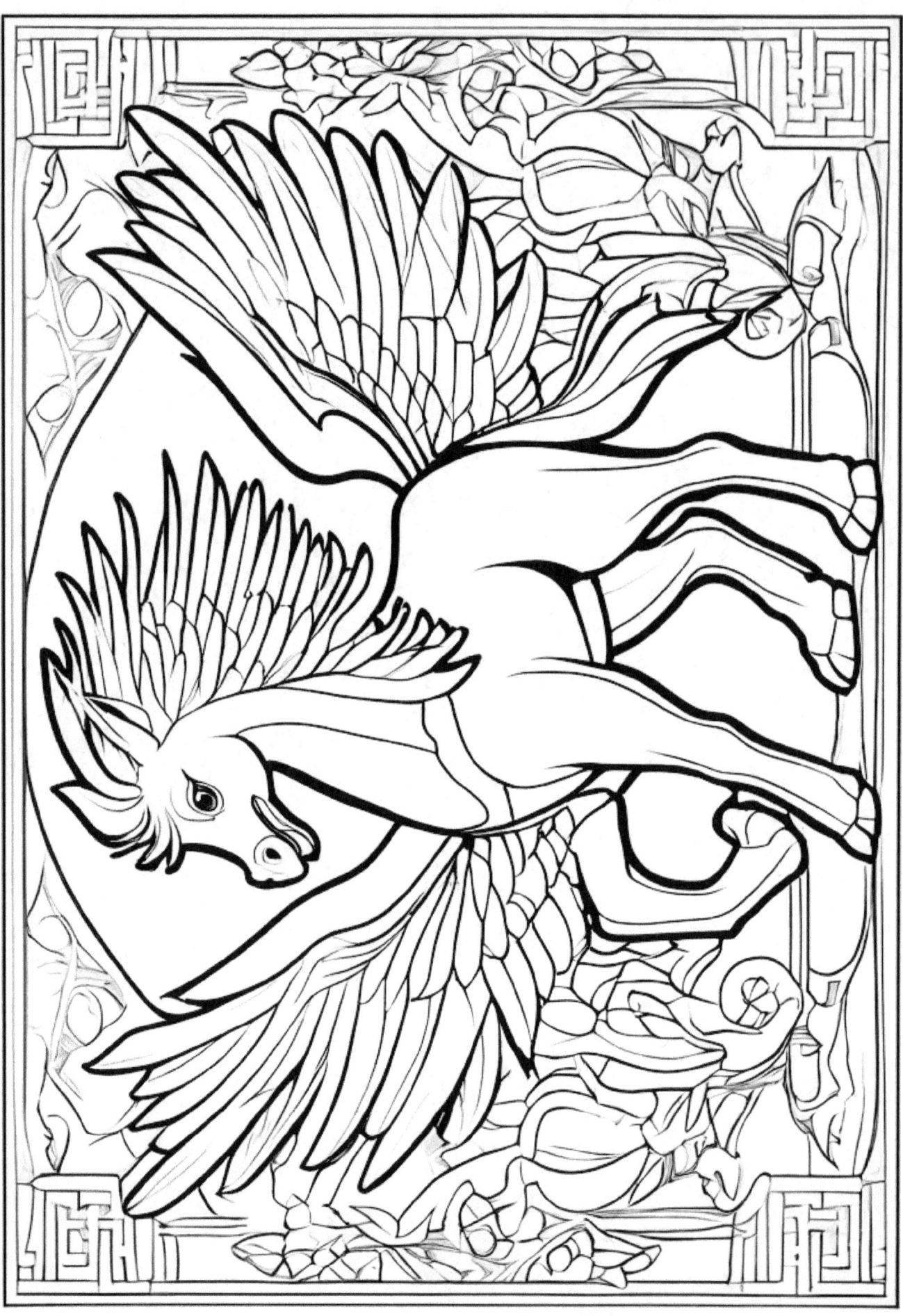

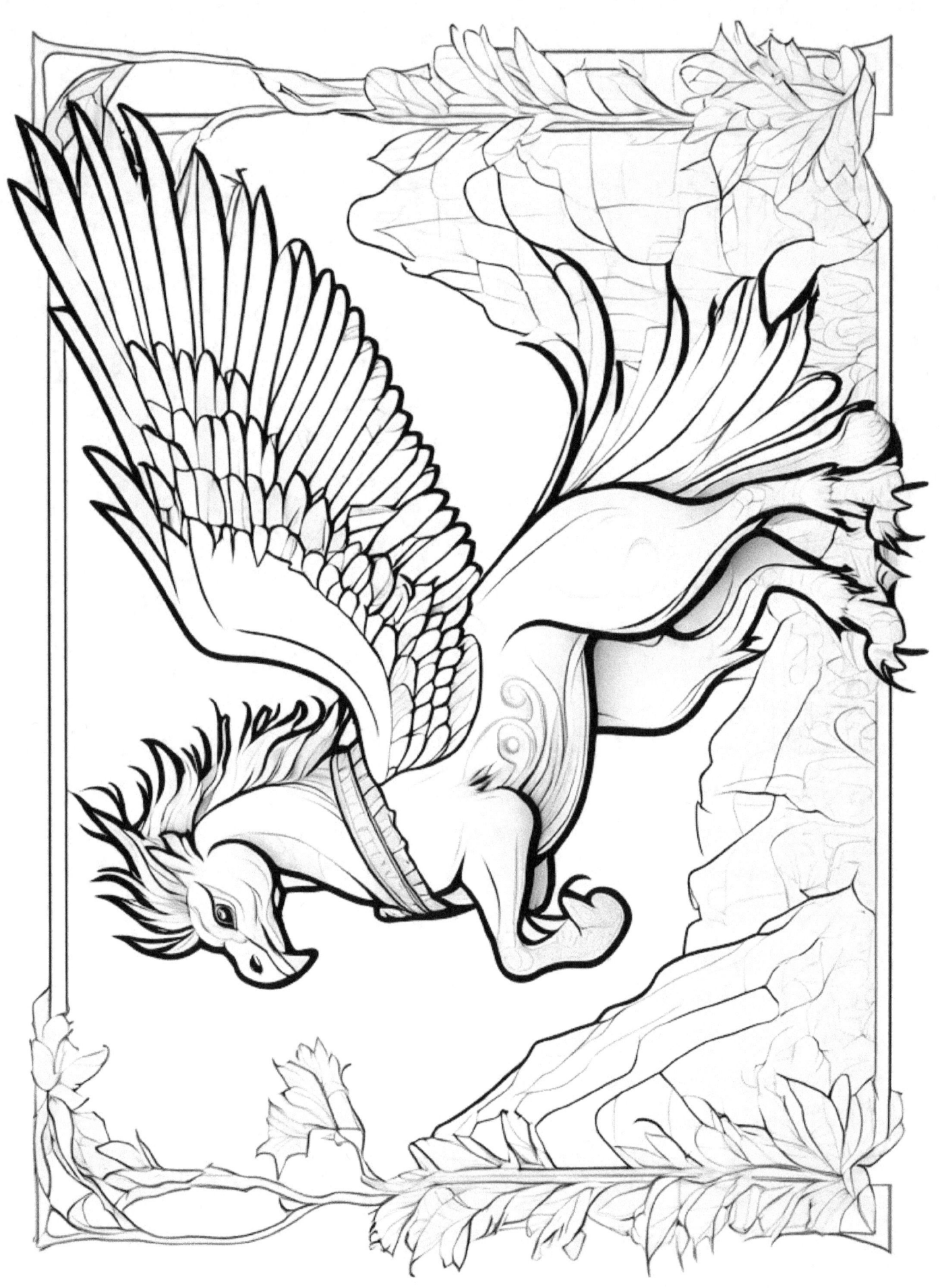

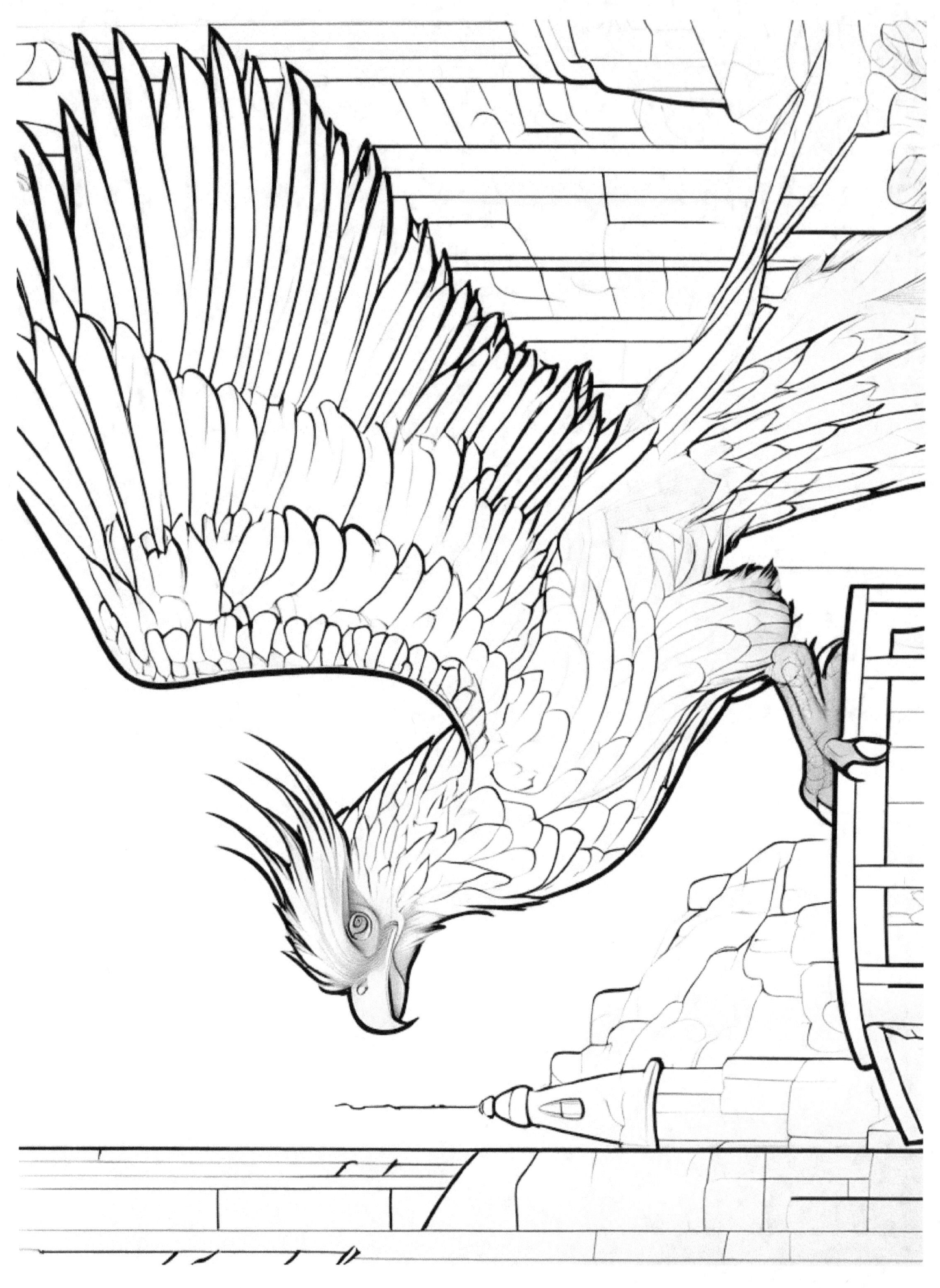

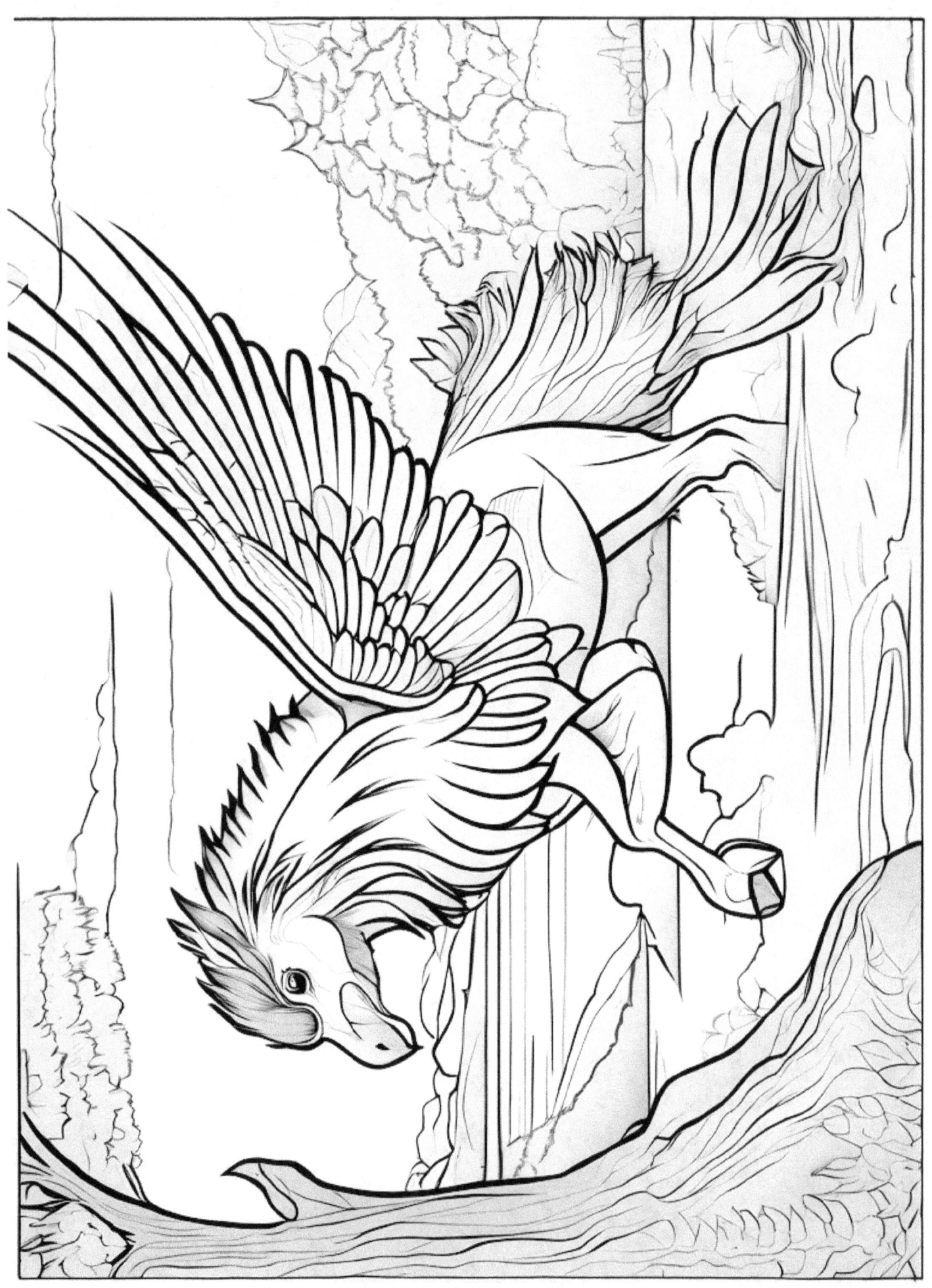

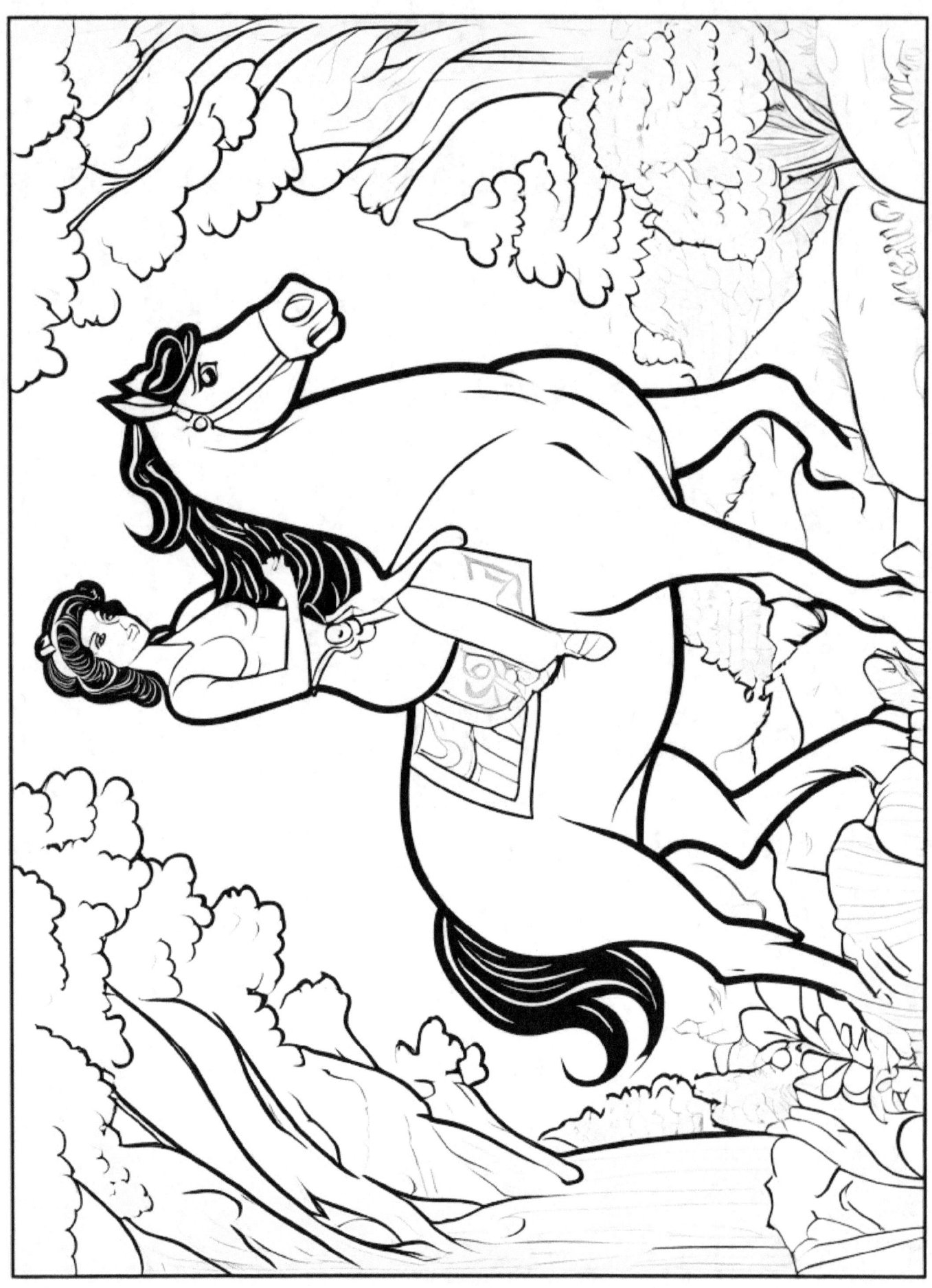

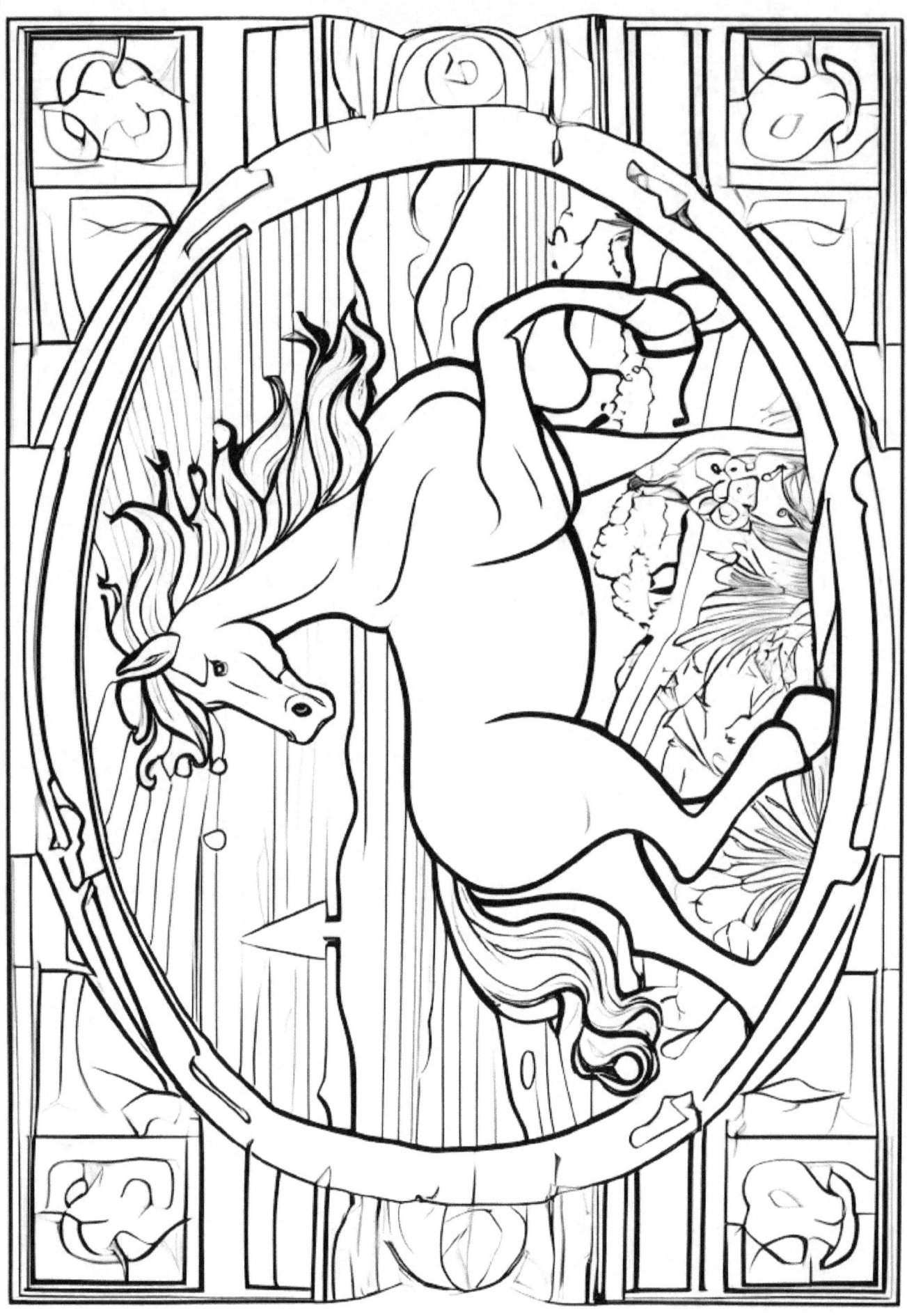

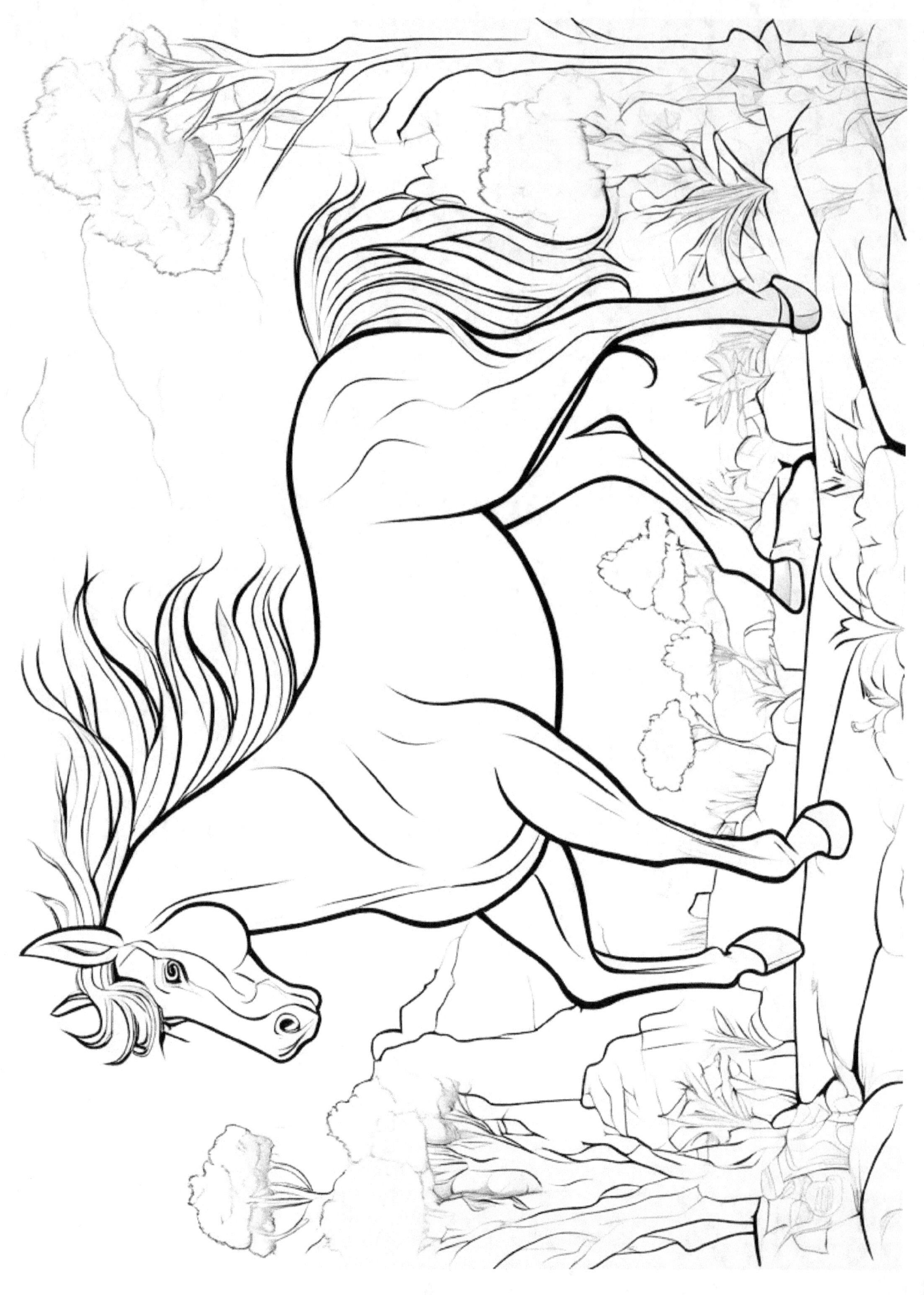

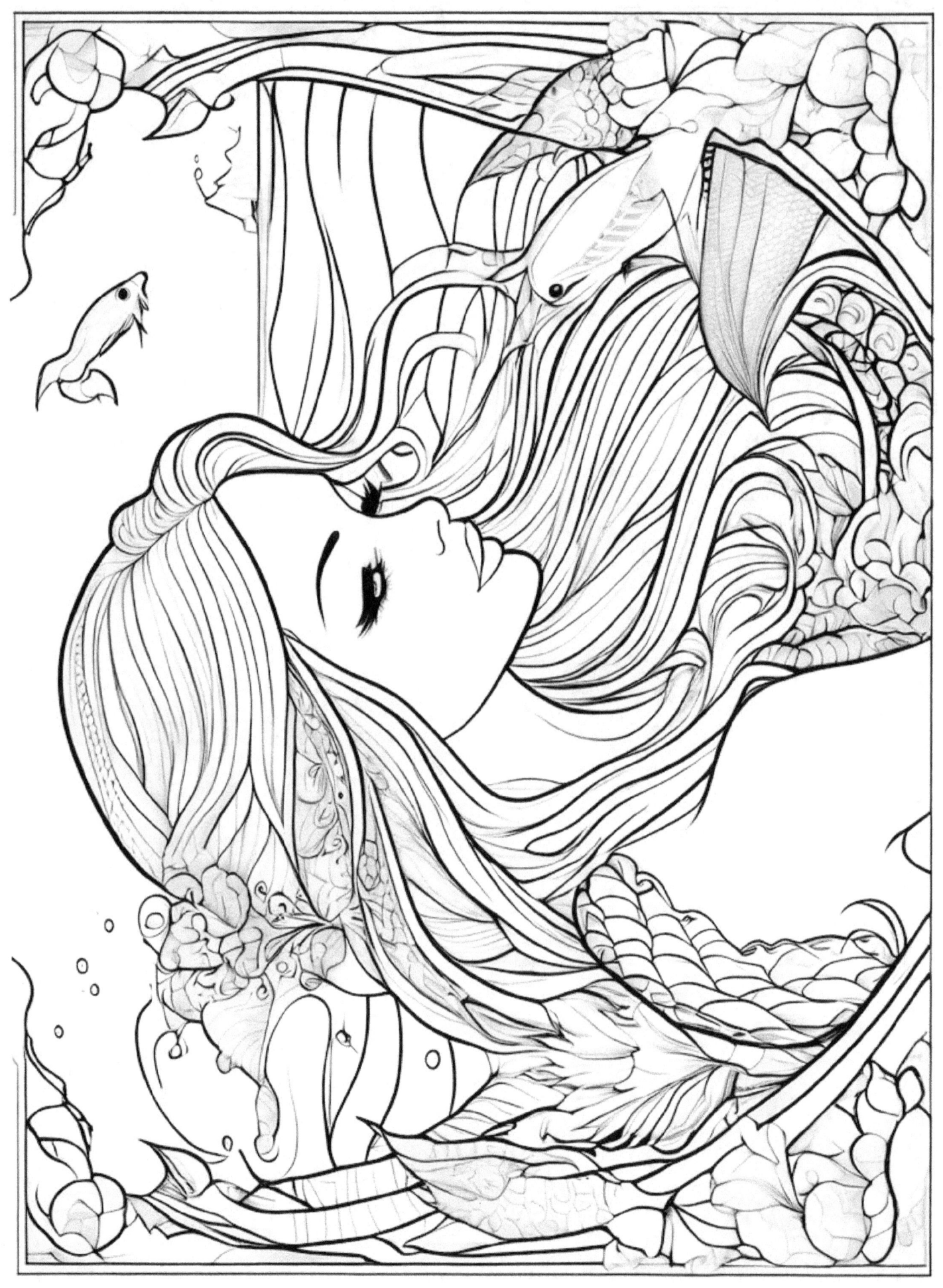

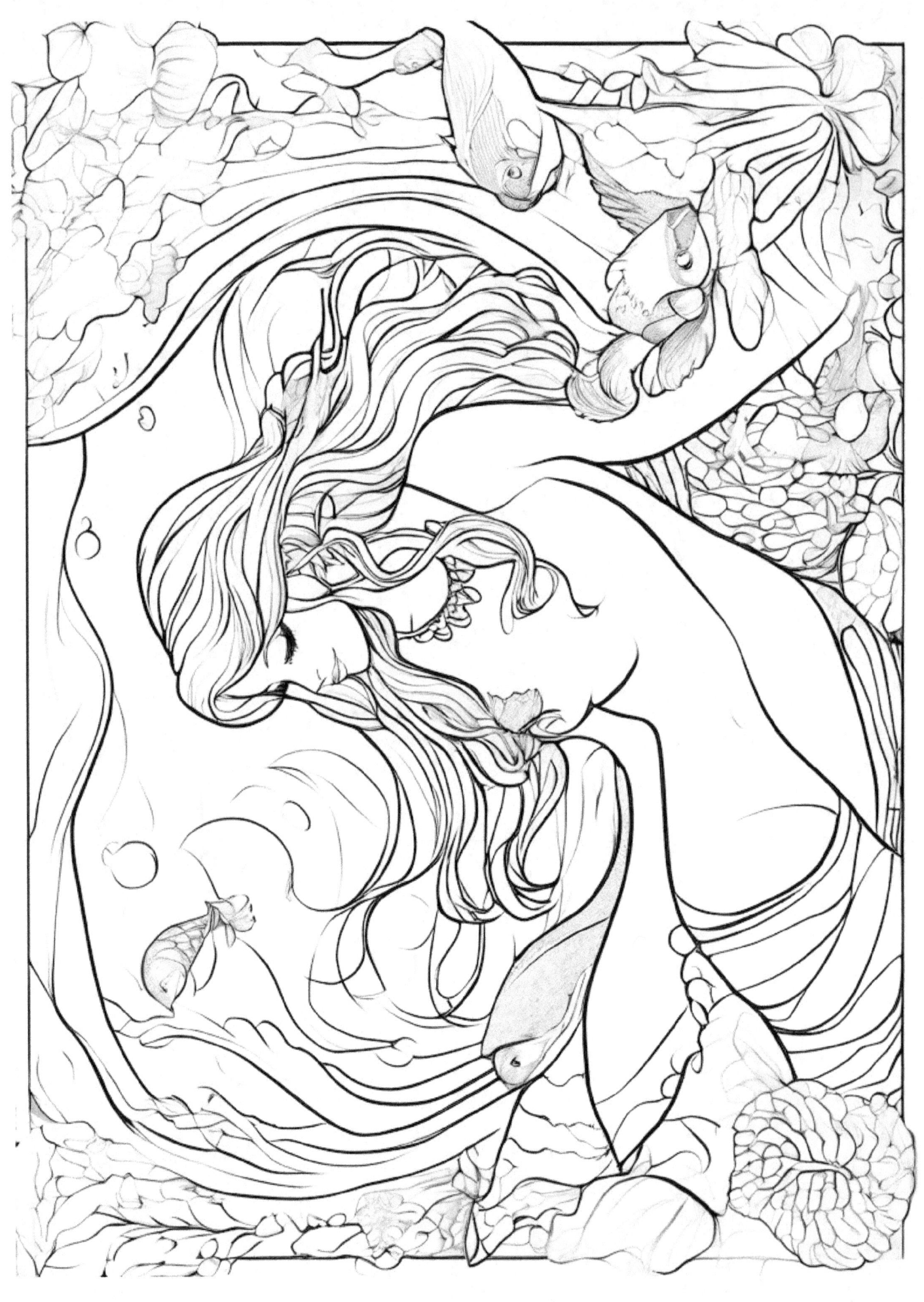

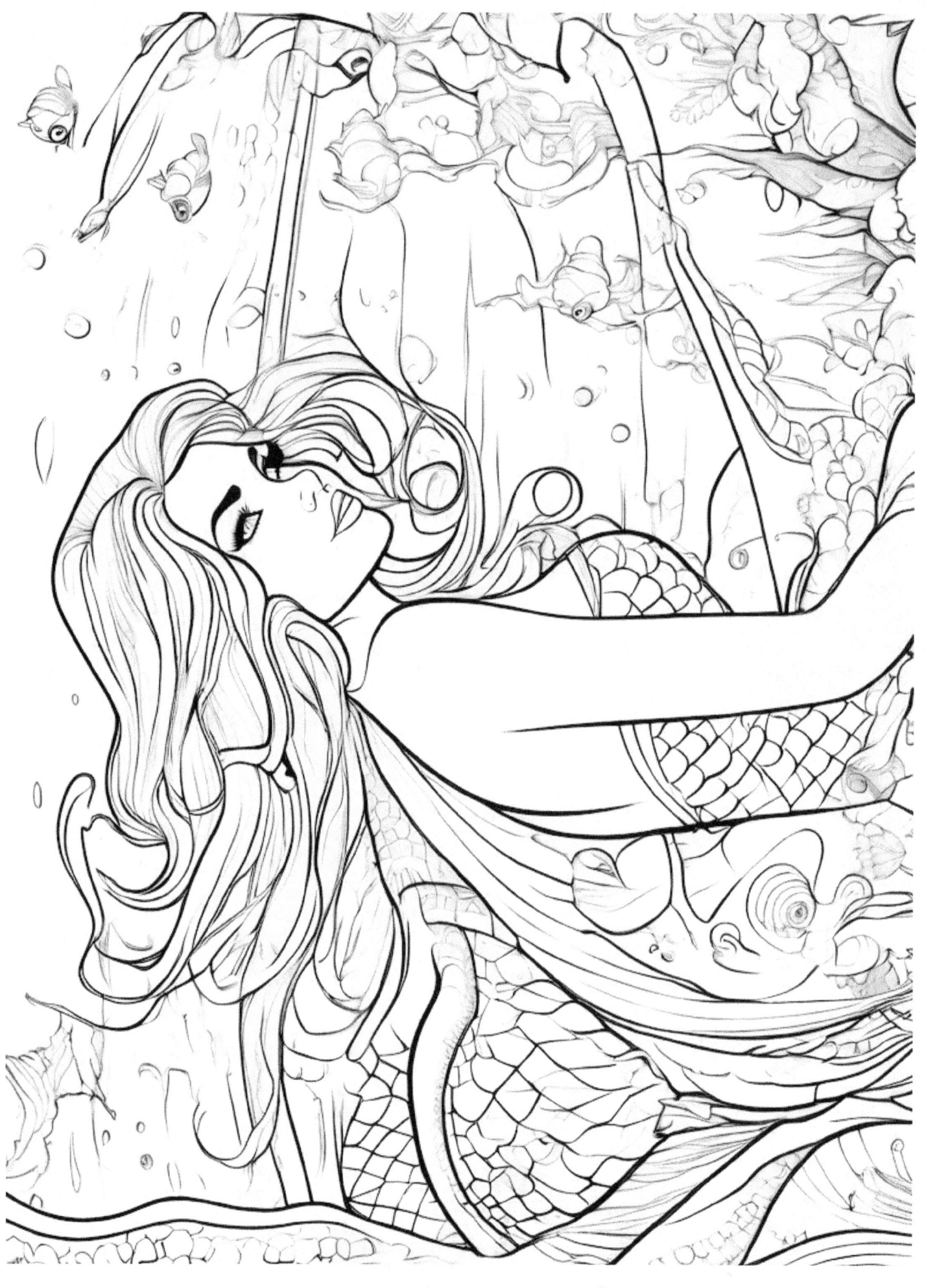

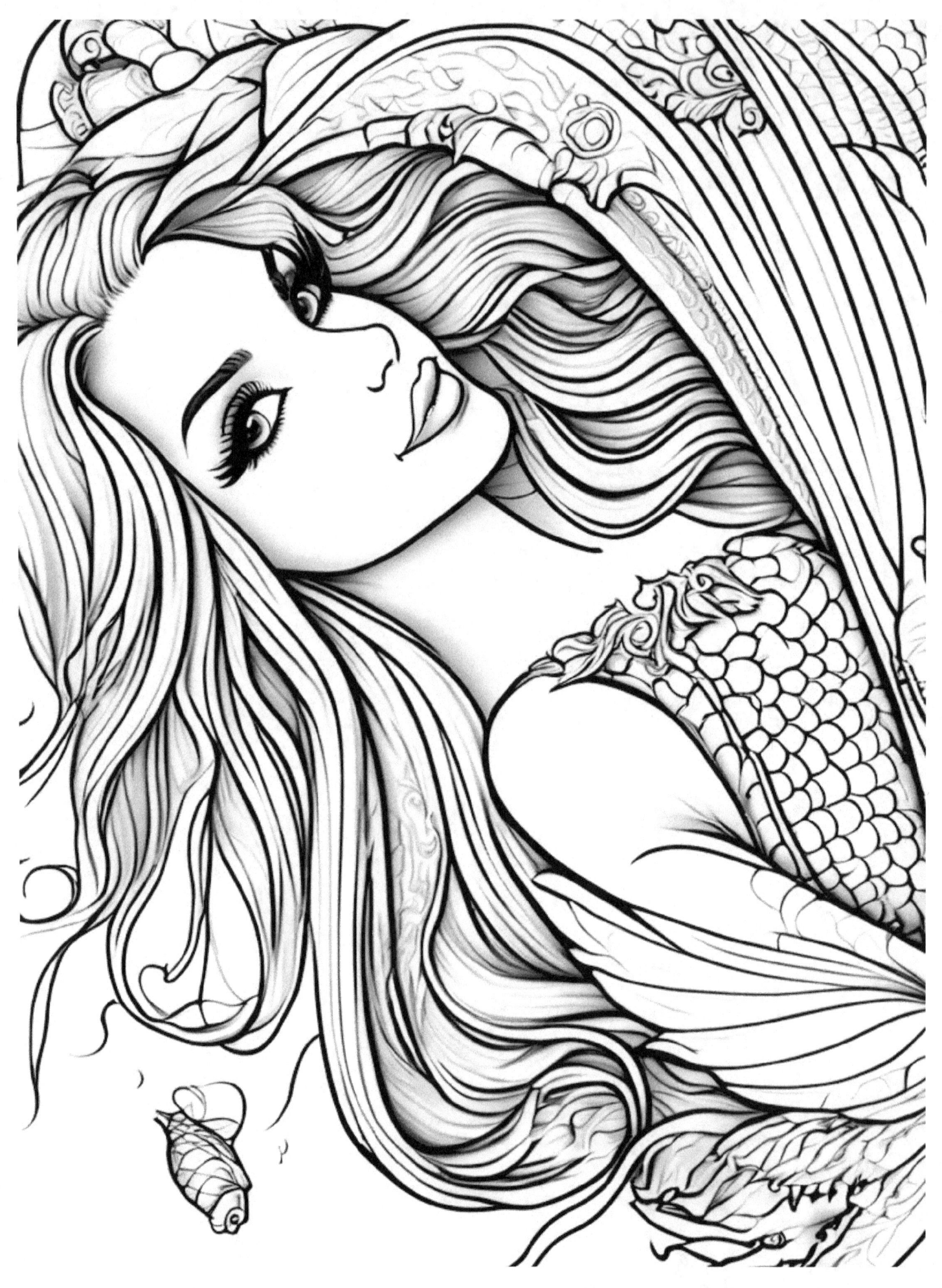

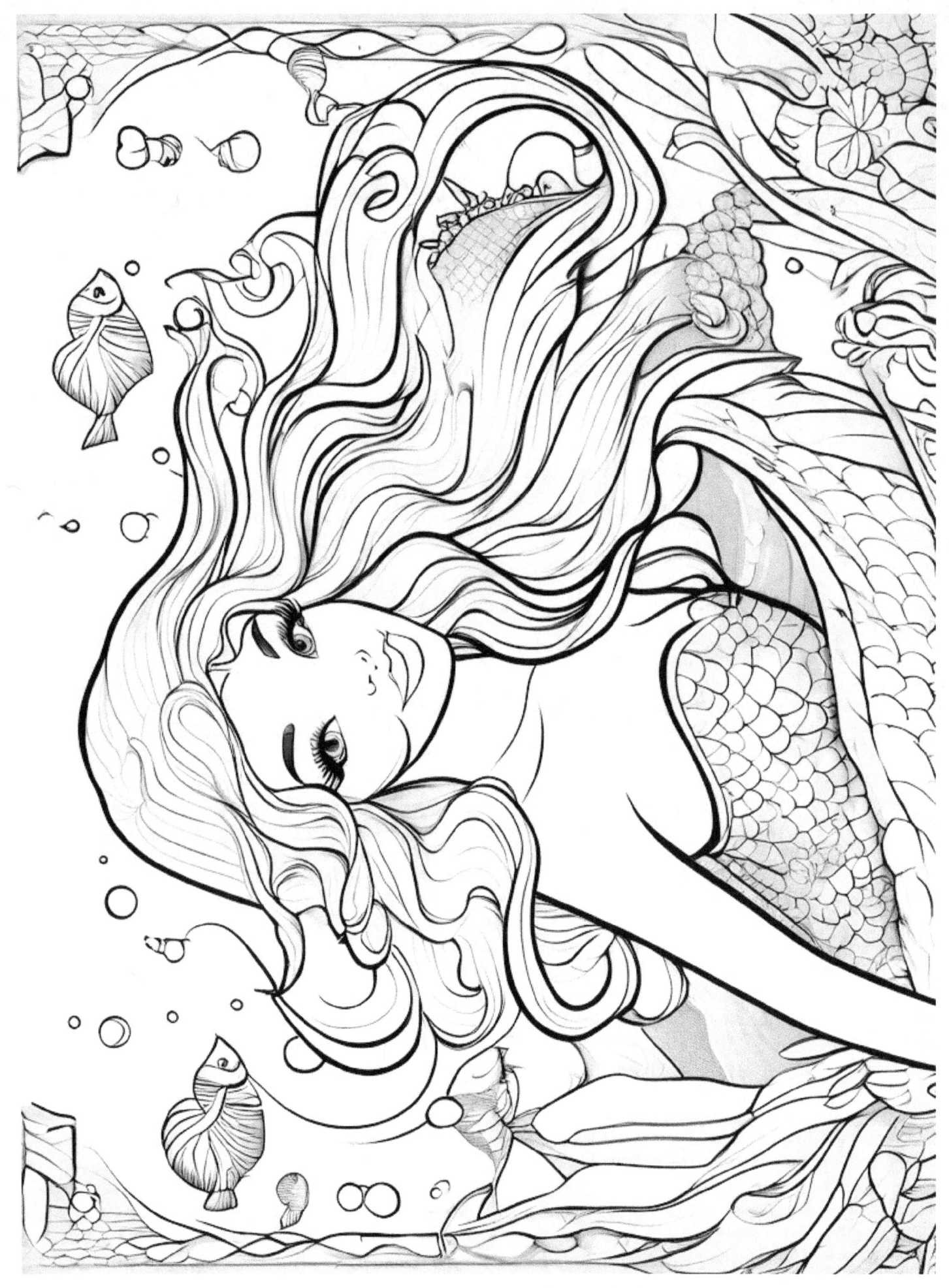

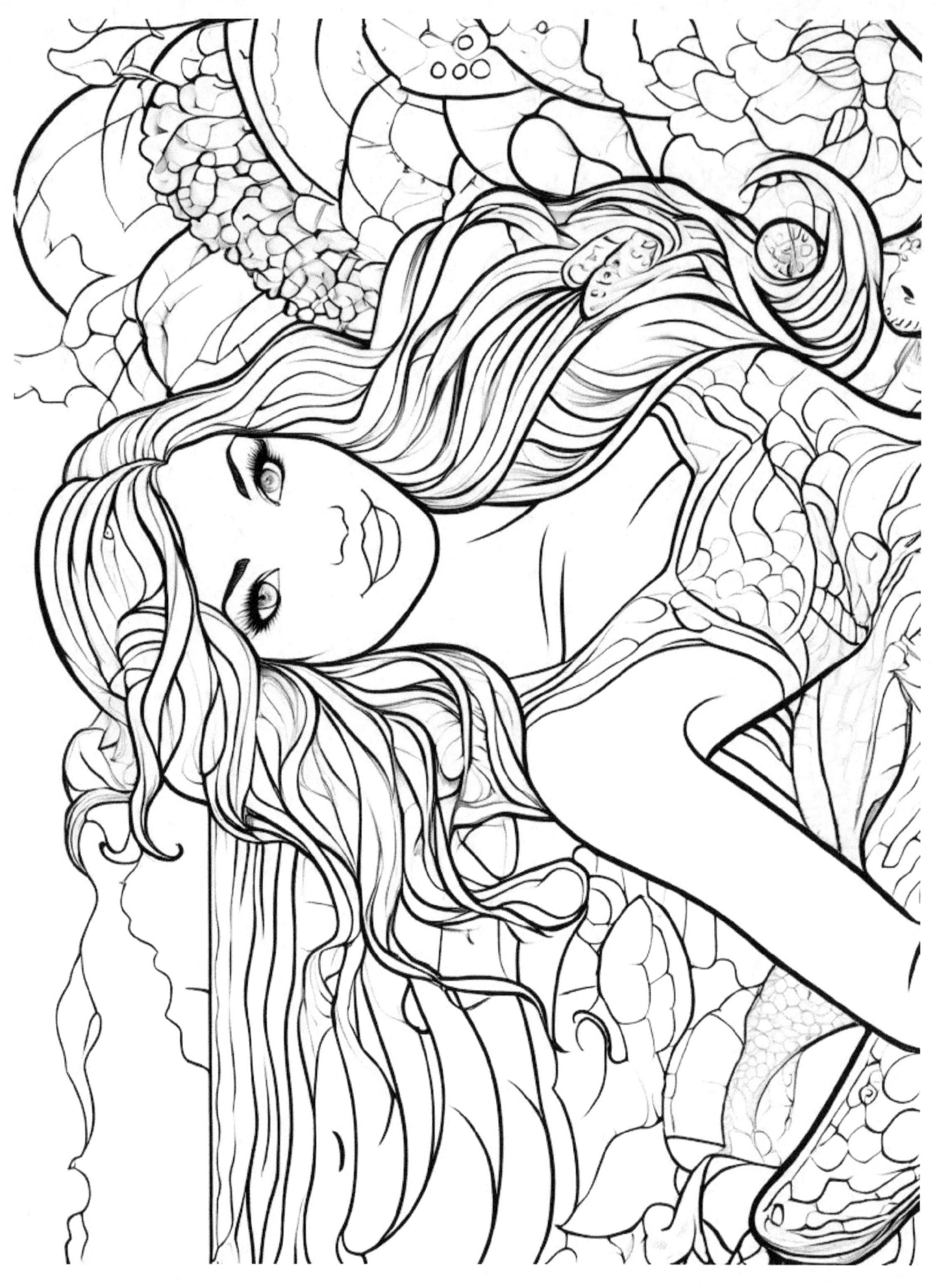

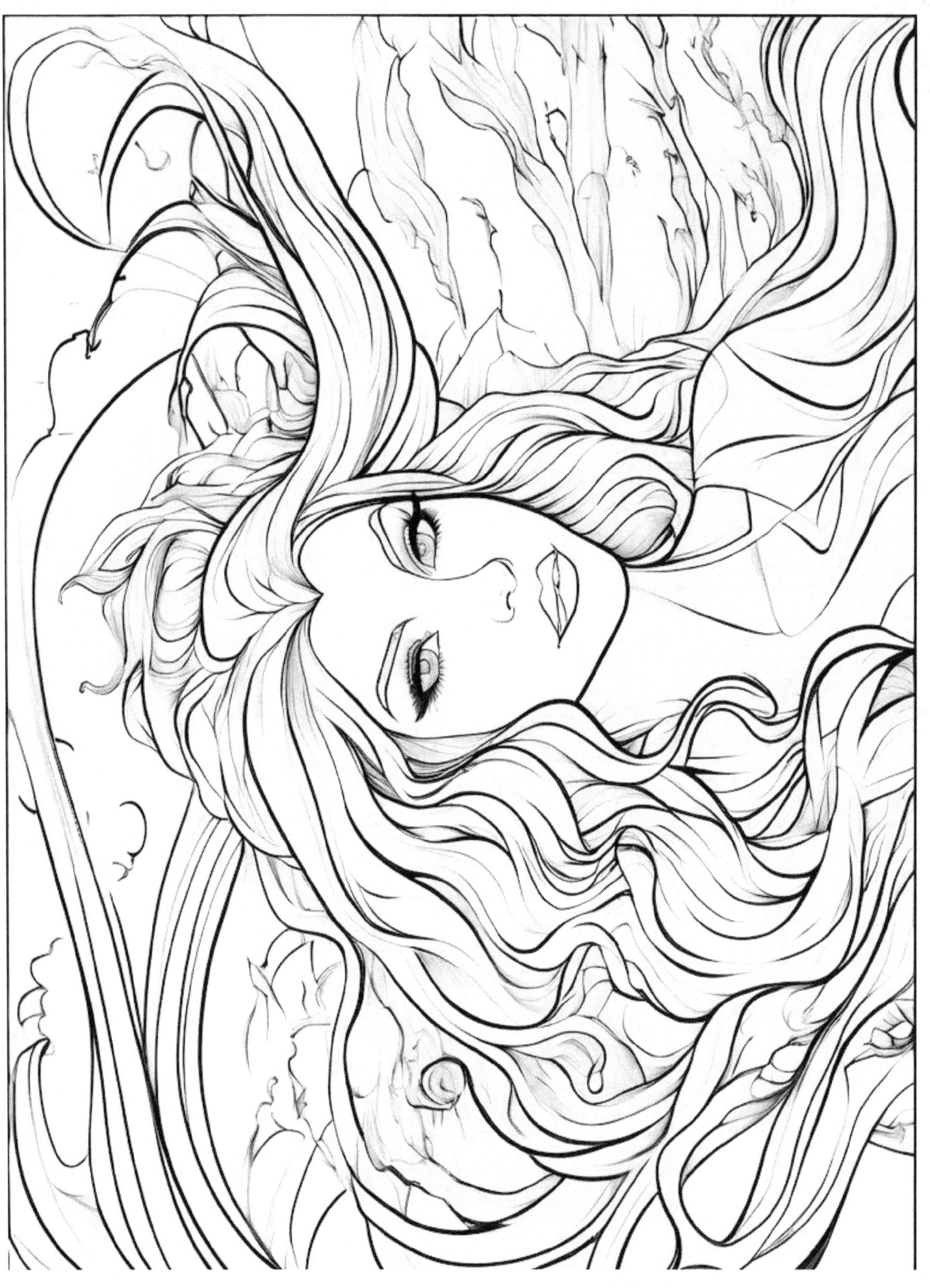

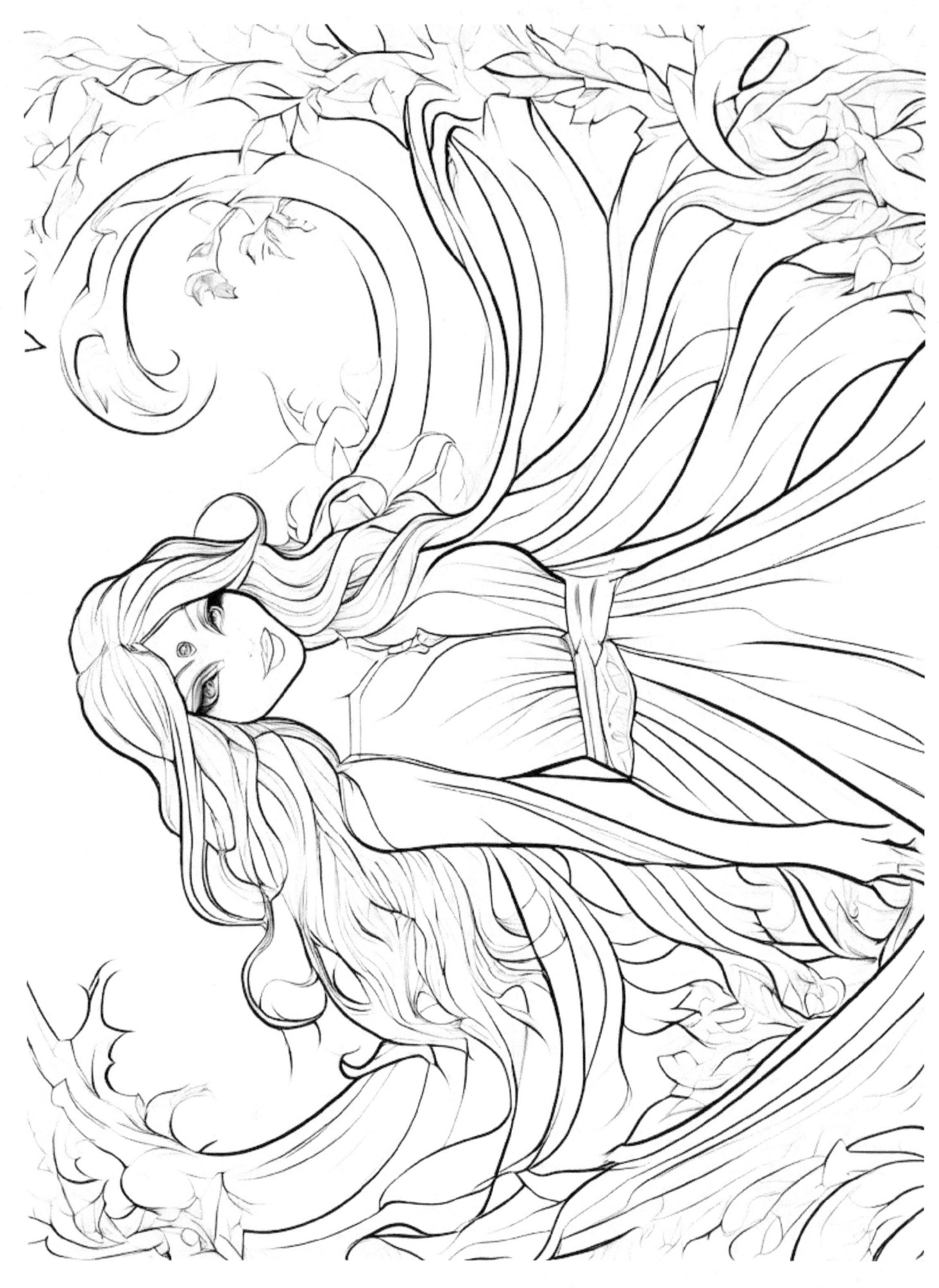

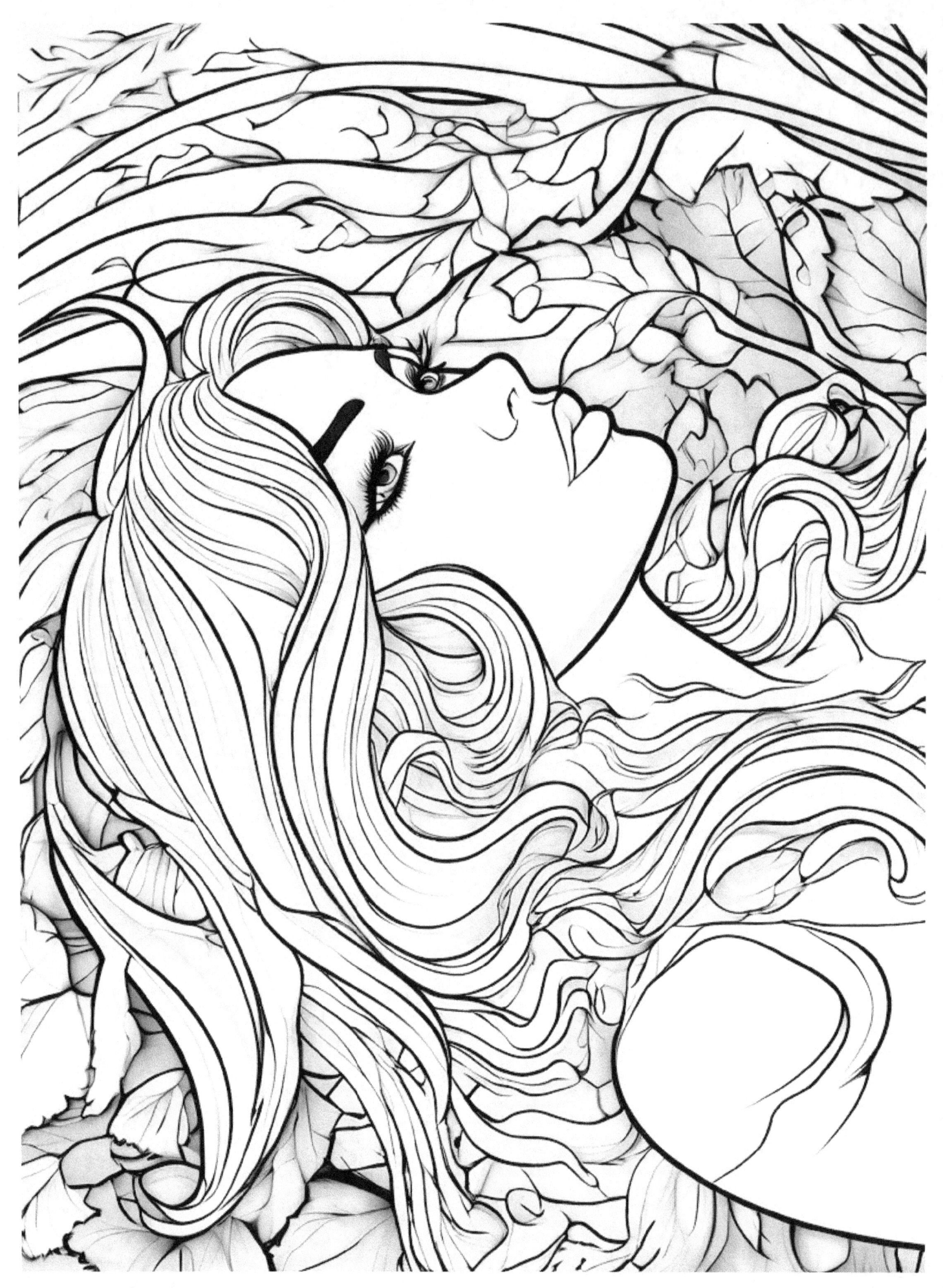

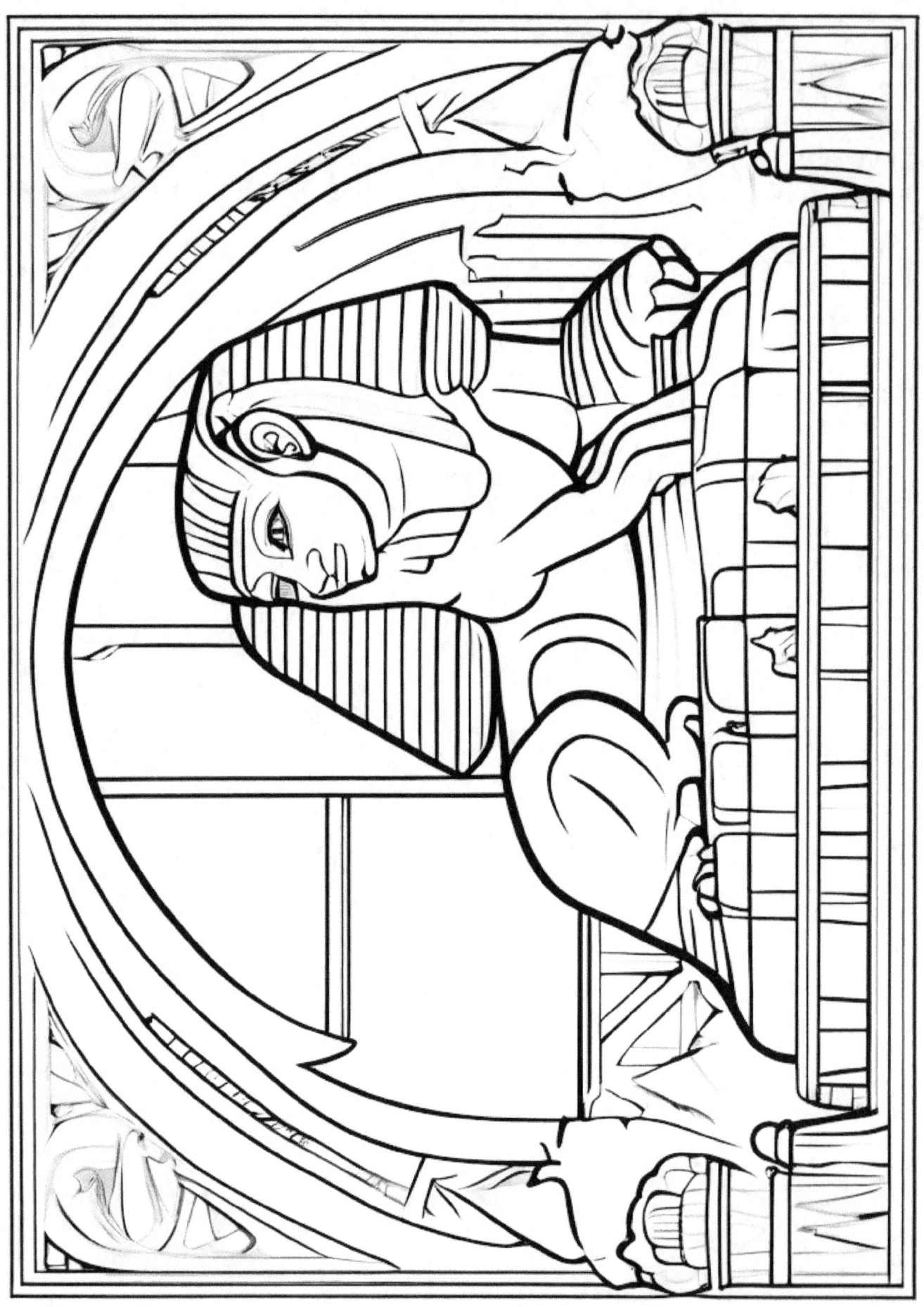

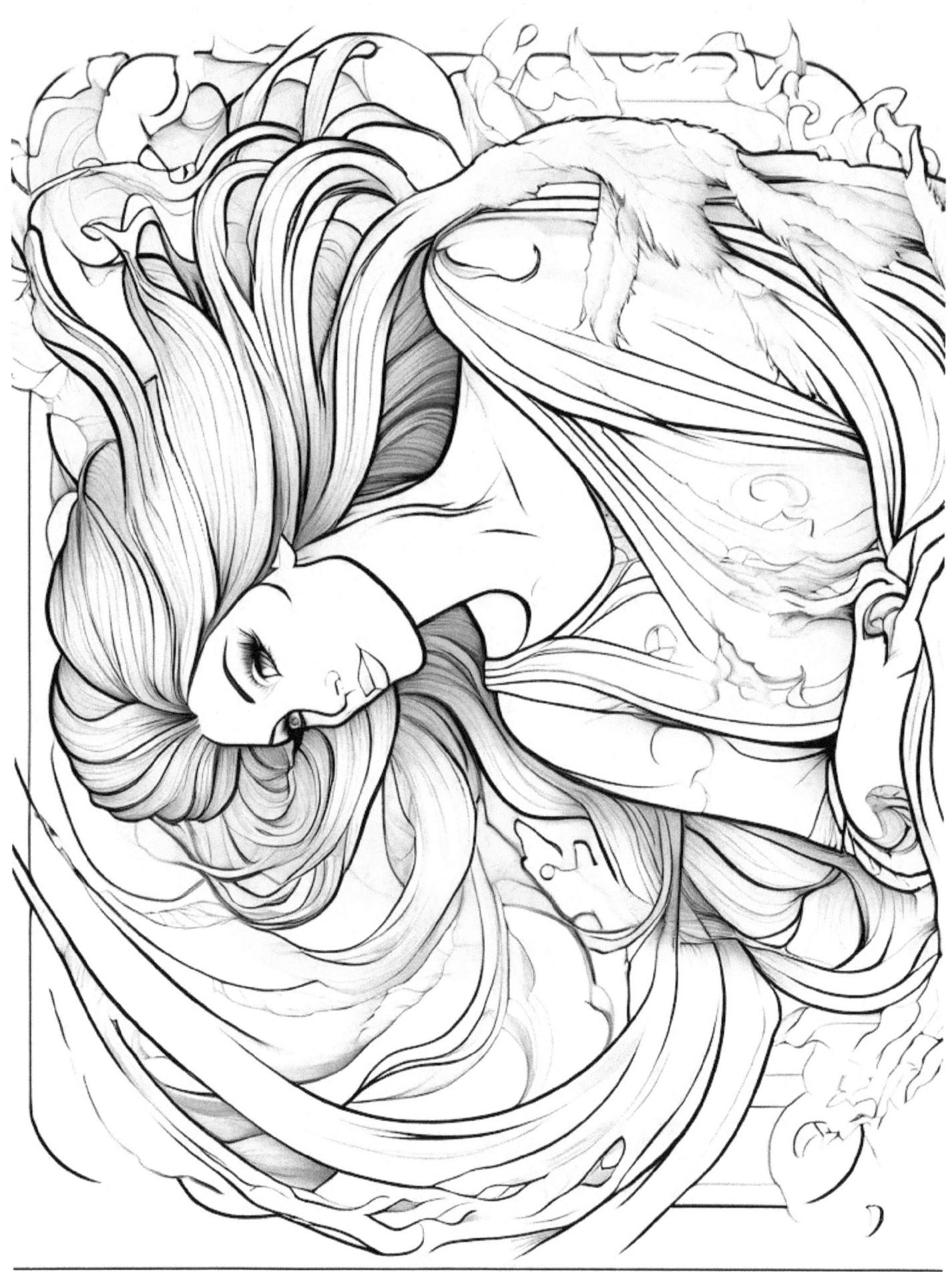

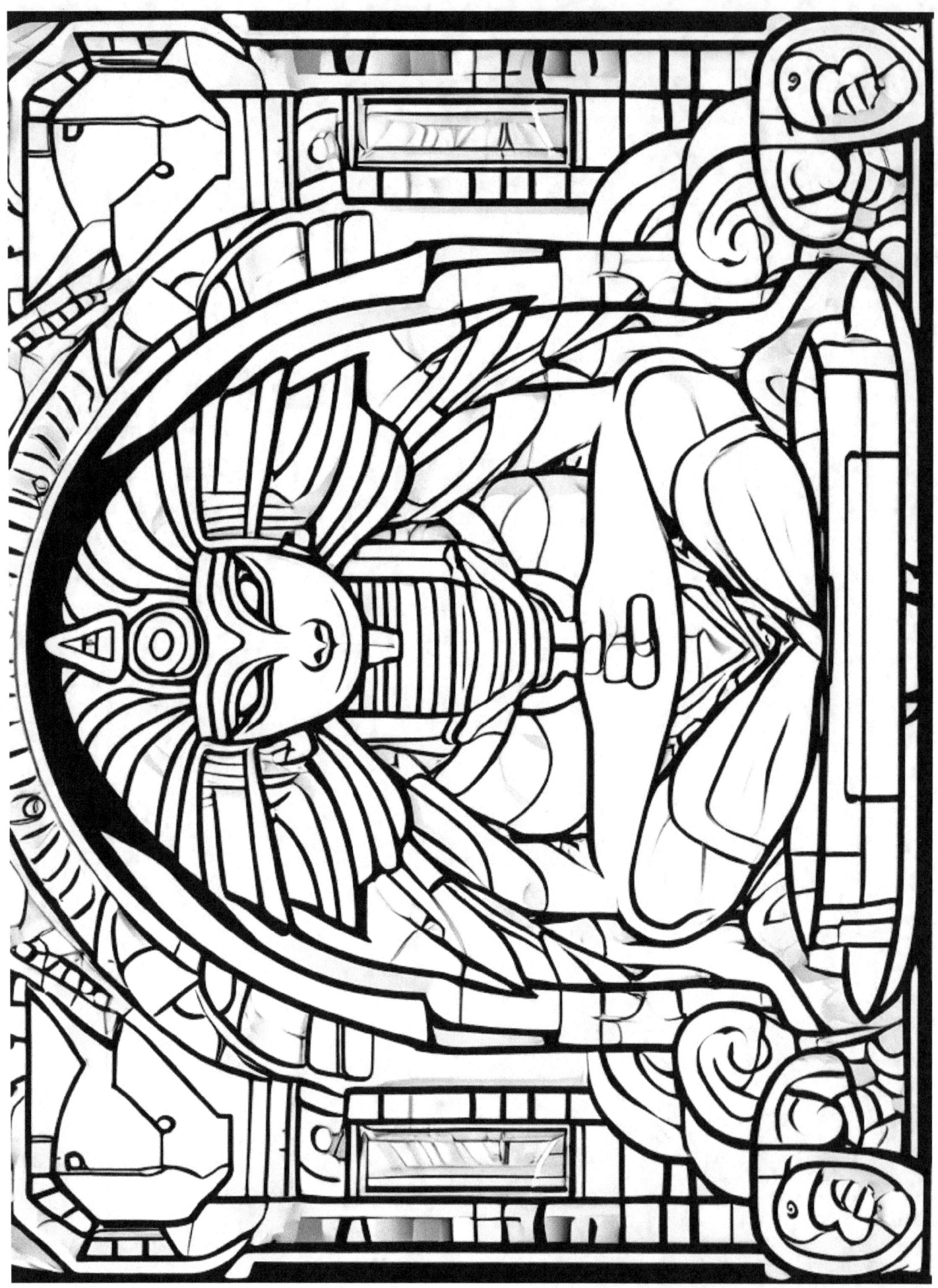

www.ingramcontent.com/pod-product-compliance
Lightning Source LLC
Chambersburg PA
CBHW082213220526
45470CB00010B/3146